Praise for Alexander Odishelidze's last book,
Pay to the Order of Puerto Rico

*"It is fitting that we ask ourselves what future political status
is best for Puerto Rico. This book answers that question and
another: What status is also best for the United States?"*

Robert J. Lagomarsino
Former US Representative of California
Ranking Member of Subcommittee on Territorial Affairs

*"Just as Art Laffer helped start a revolution of thought about
taxes on the mainland more than twenty-five years ago, he
and Alex Odishelidze will begin a national debate about the
relationship between the United States and Puerto Rico.* Pay to
the Order of Puerto Rico *is an important book for understanding
the roots and consequences of a failed economic policy."*

The Honorable Jack Kemp

*"Mr. Odishelidze's book reveals the economic and social
consequences of the confused and ambiguous territorial status
policy Congress has implemented for Puerto Rico... The sooner the
better in order to bring about an orderly culmination of Puerto
Rico's political progress from territory to a permanent status."*

Richard Thornburgh
Former United States Attorney General

AMERICA'S LAST FORTRESS

PUERTO RICO'S SOVEREIGNTY, CHINA'S CARIBBEAN BELT AND ROAD, AND AMERICA'S NATIONAL SECURITY

ALEXANDER ODISHELIDZE

Editing, design, and distribution by Bublish, Inc.

Available to bookstores and libraries through Ingram.

ISBN: 978-1-64704-513-5 (eBook)
ISBN: 978-1-64704-514-2 (paperback)
ISBN: 978-1-64704-515-9 (hardback)

Publisher's Cataloging-In-Publication Data
(Prepared by The Donohue Group, Inc.)

Names: Odishelidze, Alexander, author.
Title: America's last fortress : Puerto Rico's sovereignty, China's Caribbean Belt and
    Road, and America's national security / Alexander Odishelidze.
Description: [Puerto Rico] : [Omanagement LLC/Publishing Division], [2022] |
    Includes index.
Identifiers: ISBN 9781647045159 (hardback) | ISBN 9781647045142 (paperback) |
    ISBN 9781647045135 (ebook)
Subjects: LCSH: Puerto Rico--Foreign economic relations--China. | Puerto Rico--
    Foreign economic relations--Caribbean area. | Puerto Rico--Politics and
    government. | United States--Foreign relations--China. | Yi dai yi lu (Initiative :
    China) | National security--United States.
Classification: LCC HF1506.15.C6 O35 2022 | DDC 337.7295051--dc23

Dedication

I WANT TO THANK THOSE WHO HAVE BEEN CLOSEST TO ME DURING the process of putting out this book, my immediate family. Thank you to my wife of 25 years, Odette, who is my best friend and life-time companion. Like a real champ, she has always given me the support I've needed—both in business and in life. Also, of course, thank you to my oldest son Sasha, my younger son Michael, and most of all to my granddaughter Allie, who is a real champ in her own right through her political, social media campaigning. Kudos to our younger generation. I know they will make this world right again!

Contents

A FRONT ROW SEAT TO CHINA'S CARIBBEAN GAMBIT

I FIRST REALIZED HOW SERIOUS CHINA'S INTEREST IN PUERTO RICO was after giving a speech at the Wan Chai Rotary Club in Hong Kong in 2018. The subject of my talk was a book I had coauthored with economist Arthur Laffer, called *Pay to the Order of Puerto Rico*. It touched on various political, economic, racial, and ethnic issues on the island. Though I have made my life and money in Puerto Rico and spent the last sixty years plugged into its economy, culture, society, and politics, I am not Puerto Rican by birth. My youth was spent in Nazi-occupied Belgrade and later in Communist Yugoslavia. In 1960, at the age of nineteen, and after almost three years in European refugee camps, I landed in America with $20 in my pocket and no understanding of English. It's a long story, but many years later, I had become a successful family and businessman in Puerto Rico. Life is a fascinating journey—more on that later.

I share my Russian-who-immigrated-to-America bio because it always seems to loosen up my Chinese audiences. When I first started meeting Chinese businesspeople, I would simply tell them that I was from America. After this news, they would politely shake my hand and walk away. When I started telling them I was a Russian who immigrated to America, things changed. I would get a big smile, a hug, and be called, *tovarisch*, which in Russian means comrade. I think you get the picture. So, when I shared my Soviet-bloc background with my Hong Kong-Chinese audience during my 2018 speech, they immediately assumed we were "on the same side" and felt they could share information with me much more freely. The evening would prove to be enlightening, to say the least.

After my speech, I was surrounded by attendees asking questions. One mergers and acquisitions (M&A) professional, who'd been born in Hong Kong but was not Chinese, showed special interest in my speech. He told me that his partners were Chinese from both Hong Kong and mainland China, and they were acquiring properties for the benefit of Chinese interests. He also explained that his clients were primarily focused on acquisitions in the US and Caribbean.

"We are negotiating to buy Roosevelt Roads," he shared proudly.

It's possible my jaw physically dropped to the floor at this news. Roosevelt Roads was the original naval base established in Puerto Rico by the US government in 1943. Upgraded in 1957, the base was occasionally used by the Navy for training exercises. Mainly, though, it served as a permanent American footprint in the Caribbean for emergency defensive, quick-response maneuvers to discourage aggressive intruders during WWII and the Cold War. In the early 1960s, when Khrushchev decided to put nuclear missiles in Cuba, the blockade ordered by President John F. Kennedy was mounted out of Roosevelt Roads. The US Department of Defense once called the base "our permanent battleship in the Caribbean."

And it's not just the base itself that has been strategically important. The construction of the Roosevelt Roads naval base included substantial excavations into the surrounding mountains during World War II, when England was under heavy German attack. The facility was designed to provide Churchill and the British government safe haven should they have to exile during the blitzkrieg. And in the 1970s, the Navy claimed proudly but secretly that it had spent $4 billion on this grid system alone and that it was one of the most modern, advanced, and important training tools for naval maneuvers. Then, in the early 2000s, President George W. Bush decided that America did not need protection in the Caribbean any longer. He turned the base over to the local Puerto Rican government. Since then, the Department of Defense has pulled out of Puerto Rico almost completely. Roosevelt Roads, along with other US military installations, was put up for sale.

Once I had recovered from the shock of what my Hong Kong attendee was telling me, I tried to calmly ask, "So, what does the US government say about your deal?"

"Oh, we are not talking to the US government," The M&A professional continued. "We are dealing with the governor of Puerto Rico, who has assured us that they have complete control and do not need US permission to make this deal."

Supposedly, Puerto Rican Governor Ricardo Rosselló had told them it would be better for "political reasons" to call this venture a "tourism and industrial development project." He also advised them to submit plans that included beach condos, hotels, a boardwalk with waterside restaurants and perhaps a few stores, along with a private marina. The group was buying a fully functioning US naval base, after all, so it would be best to avoid any raised eyebrows. At the time, *Fomento*, the Puerto Rico industrial development agency, touted the sale without revealing the real purchasers.

Looking back, I wonder if my M&A colleague even knew who was behind the deal. It's quite possible he did not. According to my Hong Kong attendees, Rosselló had suggested that the Chinese pursue the acquisition through a US hedge fund as a "directed investment." This way China could invest the purchase price in the hedge fund and "direct" it to buy the naval base limiting their share of the profits. The hedge fund would get the fees for the acquisition and China would get the property without their name attached to it—creating the appearance of a domestic US acquisition. Of course, with China's permission, the original hedge fund could profitably sell this "directed investment" to another investor through a separate corporate entity or hedge fund, and so on. Eventually, the identities of the original purchasers would be lost in the mountains of paperwork these transactions require.

When I left the Wan Chai Rotary Club that day, I started looking deeper into the Roosevelt Roads project, and heard rumors that confirmed what I'd been told in Hong Kong. Apparently, Governor Rosselló—the son of former Governor Pedro Rosselló, who had been responsible for getting the Department of Defense out of Puerto Rico a decade earlier—had turned over many classified documents relating to the former US naval base in order to smooth over the sale of Roosevelt Roads. It's probably not a coincidence that two years after he was elected, the people of Puerto Rico marched on the governor's house and successfully removed him from office, even though he still had two years remaining in his term.

Though I was stunned by the circumstances of the deal, I was not at all surprised by China's interest in Roosevelt Roads. It is definitely a prize piece of real estate. The bay where the base once sat is surrounded by mountains and ringed by beautiful beach areas on its seashore. Just a few miles from the bay lies the gorgeous island of Culebra, which is home to one of the most beautiful beaches in the world. But the crystal-clear waters around Culebra are not as pristine as they appear. Culebra was once consistently bombarded by missiles launched as target practice from naval vessels based at Roosevelt Roads. I will never forget the first time I sailed around Culebra. When I looked at the charts, I saw warning signs everywhere saying, "Danger! Unexploded Ordnance!" This, of course, stifled my desire to jump into those fabulous, reef-rich waters full of fish and lobsters.

Though the involved parties claimed the objective of the Roosevelt Roads deal was economic rather than geopolitical, the fact that a strategic US naval base could be sold to a foreign adversary seemed unthinkable to me. The infrastructure of that base could be used at any time, by anyone controlling that piece of real estate, no matter how many McDonalds, Marriotts, and Holiday Inns could be erected to line the beach. The greater danger was that Roosevelt Roads military infrastructure would no longer be available to the US military to launch any operations against potential enemies who challenged the US in the Caribbean. With China controlling much of the rest of the Caribbean, America would not have a place to launch a blockade to stop unwanted visitors with nefarious intentions, as we did during the Kennedy years.

We find ourselves in this surprising situation for many reasons, but primarily due to China's Belt and Road Initiative—a long-term infrastructure investment plan to create an unbroken trade route for Chinese goods to circle the world without interference from any other country. If it is successful, the plan would be a geopolitical masterstroke, setting up China for the same kind of soft-power status in the twenty-first century that Britain and America enjoyed in the nineteenth and twentieth centuries, respectively. Right now, China's main trade route begins in Beijing. A railroad connection through Siberia and Russia brings Chinese goods to Europe, and then from Paris via the Chunnel, they wind up in London. From the UK, Chinese goods are loaded onto ships for the transatlantic voyage. But this northern route relies too heavily on western influence. In case a conflict were to arise, China would need an alternative. Enter the Mediterranean port in Syria.

Bashar al-Assad, president of Syria, is backed by both Russia and Iran. So, as part of their strategic alliance, Iran and Russia have pledged to help China develop a secure passage to Syria's Mediterranean port. For those who wonder why Assad, after all his atrocities, is still in power, this is the answer: Anyone who dares take him out will have to deal with China, Russia, Iran, and their client states, which right now may be more powerful militarily than NATO when you consider their combined resources—especially in the wake of Donald Trump's isolationist presidency. Europe can no longer depend on the US to bail them out, so if there is a conflict with China's allies in the Middle East, Europe will probably stay out of it.

Once Chinese ships are loaded in either Syria or England, they need to get through the Panama Canal (or the new canal China is building in Nicaragua) in order to reach the Pacific Ocean and complete their worldwide trade route. But in order to get to Panama, they must pass through Puerto Rico, which is still the domain of China's natural enemy, the United States of America. As long as Puerto Rico is a US territory without sovereignty, Congress can still step in and prevent a foreign military presence—effectively, cutting off access to China's Belt and Road Initiative.

But how long will colonial status last for Puerto Rico in today's modern world? Most other former colonies have already gained their independence. Economic interests are the main drivers of foreign influence today, rather than a military occupation. This is precisely why the Chinese have such an interest in Puerto Rico. From what I have learned in my visits to Asia and speaking to groups of Chinese businessmen, it is in the best interest of China to try to transition Puerto Rico away from US statehood and toward national independence. Once that is achieved, Chinese investments there can pour in, quickly turning Puerto Rico into another client state—just like so many other Caribbean and Latin American nations.

Puerto Rico is currently the only part of Latin America—which includes the northern nations of South America, all of Central America, and the Caribbean islands—that has not yet been openly and heavily influenced by the Chinese. In the past decade alone, China has pumped hundreds of billions of dollars of investments into the region. Since Panama officially signed on to the Belt and Road Initiative, four new bridges across the Panama Canal have been announced. China loaned Venezuela more than $67 billion before halting investments there in 2016 due to international pressure. Cuba, China's second largest partner after Venezuela, had billions of dollars of debt written off by Chinese investors. The biggest potential winner in the region may be Nicaragua, which has been floated as a site for a new Chinese-financed canal project that would be a major counter to the US dominance of the Panama Canal. Why would China invest so heavily in the Caribbean and its surrounding countries and not invest in Puerto Rico? Because they can't, due to Puerto Rico's status as a US colony. Strategically, Puerto Rico would be China's most important prize because it blocks the entrance to the Panama Canal through the southern Caribbean.

It's conceivable that the Chinese could offer the US a boatload of cash to take possession of Puerto Rico and its people. This may seem far-fetched, but it is perfectly legal under current US law. In 2016, the US Supreme Court ruled that Puerto Rico was an unincorporated territory—a possession—and that America could do whatever it damn well pleased with the island. If it wanted to sell Puerto Rico to China, along with its three million plus residents, then so be it. Some of our recent presidents might very well have considered such an offer. Former President Donald Trump, from what I have heard, tried to do that very thing. He offered to sell Puerto Rico to Denmark in return for Greenland. Investment in Puerto Rico as an independent sovereign nation might carry a fraction of the price tag of such a negotiated purchase, though. The Chinese are surely monitoring the election trends in Puerto Rico to see whether the number of Puerto Ricans voters who prefer a non-statehood candidate for governor will continue to grow as it has over the last ten years—and they will likely encourage that rising sentiment. China's goal, of course, is an independent Puerto Rico. Thirsty for money to solve its fiscal problems, an independent Puerto Rico would surely look at China as its savior from the "Yankee dollar." Right now, as much as half of Puerto Rico's fiscal budget is from US federal transfers. Money that Puerto Rico does not have must come from somewhere, if the island is to function—unless, of course, Puerto Rico decides to become another Haiti and go it totally alone. For so many reasons, this does not seem likely.

The big problem for China may come if and when the US wakes up and realizes that China is knocking at its back door. Interestingly, an April 16, 2020, press release from the office of US Congresswoman Jenniffer González-Colón, who represents Puerto Rico in Congress, stated:

> Today, US Secretary of Commerce Wilbur Ross announced that the Department's Economic Development Administration (EDA) is awarding a $4.5 million grant to the Local Redevelopment Authority for Roosevelt Roads, San Juan, Puerto Rico, to rehabilitate a building and make other infrastructure improvements on former Naval Station Roosevelt Roads. The EDA grant will support early-stage businesses focused on the visitor economy and is expected to create 134 jobs and spur $1.5 million in private investment. The project, to be located in a Tax Cuts and Jobs Act designated Opportunity Zone, will be matched with $1.25 million in local funds.

> "The Trump administration is committed to assisting Puerto Rico as they work to recover from the 2017 hurricanes," said Secretary of Commerce Wilbur Ross. "The redevelopment of the Roosevelt Roads Naval Station will bring businesses back to a vital waterfront area."

> "This investment will rehabilitate Roosevelt Road's Port Control Building for use as a multi-tenant, commercial space that will house early-stage tourism businesses," said Dana Gartzke, Performing the Delegated Duties of the Assistant Secretary of Commerce for Economic Development. "The project will also improve streets and sidewalks to facilitate pedestrian and vehicle traffic between the commercial site and the ferry terminal, and the project's location in an Opportunity Zone will encourage additional business development."

Could this be a sign that America is awakening to the Chinese threat in Puerto Rico? It's hard to be sure. But whatever presence the Chinese may now have in Puerto Rico is cloaked in secrecy and structured through hedge funds and alternate investors, so it is very difficult to determine who the real principals really are. This secrecy and subterfuge are driven by the simple fact that Puerto Rico is a US "possession," and, therefore, it behooves the Chinese to keep a very low investment profile on the island. Of course, this would be especially true if the Chinese really did put a deal together to buy a fully functioning American naval base in Puerto Rico, as I was told by the people I met after my speech in Hong Kong in 2018. There is "general awareness" that the Chinese own some hotel properties in Puerto Rico, specifically the Caribe Hilton hotel in the Condado. When walking the streets of San Juan, you can see Asian families walking in and out of their homes in the old city as well as their condos in Isle Verde, the Condado, and other locations throughout the island. Perhaps they are all just tourists—who knows?

The big question is: If we look at the issue of Puerto Rico decolonization geopolitically, would Puerto Rico be better off as a "possession" of the US or a debtor to China for all the infrastructure, utilities, and development ventures they would offer an independent Puerto Rico?

It is obvious Puerto Rico can't be both. Once again, the people of Puerto Rico will be asked to choose. Will they become an independent nation and take the "free" money offered by China? Or will they prefer continued "free" money from America as US citizens, while still remaining a colony?

"Give me liberty or give me death" was the battle cry of America's independence movement. For Puerto Rico, though, there is little liberty as a US colony and perhaps will be even less as an independent country dependent on Chinese investment dollars and debt. American statehood offers another alternative, but recent elections indicate dwindling interest in pro-statehood candidates. Since the

2020 elections confirm this trend, the chances of Puerto Rico having another shot at statehood are probably "slim to none."

It's not only a pivotal moment for Puerto Rico, but for America. If a decision is made by Congress to grant sovereignty to Puerto Rico without statehood, China will be free to openly invest there to its hearts content. The implications of such a scenario are unnerving for America's strategic security, to say the least. Whether US leadership likes it or not, Puerto Rico is America's last fortress in the Caribbean and it's time to understand what's at stake in the island's sovereignty debate.

HOW WE CAME TO
THIS CROSSROAD

THOUGH I AM NOT PUERTO RICAN BY BIRTH, I HAVE BEEN MARRIED TO Puerto Rican ladies. My children, Michael and Sasha, are as much Puerto Rican as any other ethnic mixture that they might have inherited from their parents. And though Spanish is my fourth language—after Russian, Serbo-Croatian, and English—I have, over the years, picked up a distinctively Puerto Rican accent.

Professionally, I have been in business in Puerto Rico for more than half a century and still am to this day. In the late 1970s, I started my own insurance and securities operations from scratch in Puerto Rico. By 1985, I had more than 300 people in my operation, including employees, full-time insurance agents, and securities brokers. I operated out of three offices in Puerto Rico and one in the US Virgin Islands. Aetna bought out my operations that same year.

Politically, I have been involved in the decolonization movement for more than thirty years. I have written newspaper columns, newsletters, and books about Puerto Rico. I have personally met with influential members of the US Congress in Washington, DC, including Trent Lott, Tom Daschle, Hillary Clinton, and President Joe Biden. While up to my eyeballs in politics, my book *Pay to the Order of Puerto Rico* exposed big pharma congressional influence to keep Puerto Rico a colony so that they could continue enjoying billions of dollars of tax credits. The book also described my efforts to launch a bill in the House of Representatives to create a pathway for Puerto Rican statehood. Known as the Young Bill, it passed the House by one vote but never made it through the Senate. For more than a half century, the question whether Puerto Rico should become a US state has hung like a cloud over the island's politics. Despite multiple referendums and millions of dollars spent, Puerto Rico's territorial status has changed very little since 1917.

There are many reasons why statehood efforts have repeatedly failed, but the most important reason may be that many of the influential local businesspeople who publicly say that they would like to see Puerto Rico become a state don't actually want that to happen. Statehood would mean paying federal income taxes, which could hinder the profitability of their businesses. Worse, still in their eyes, the wealthy may be forced to pay estate taxes, removing a key source of income that Puerto Rican families have been dependent on for generations. While I respect their capitalist tendencies, it's hard to swallow their hypocrisy. That accusation may seem a little extreme to some, so let me take a step back and explain how I got here. I don't pretend to be an expert on Puerto Rico's decolonization movement, but in the 1980s, I was enlisted by a group of wealthy Puerto Ricans (mostly Republicans) to help organize lobbying the United States Congress for statehood. My background as a European emigrant and financial adviser seemed to make me an ideal candidate. I was the "non–Puerto Rican" Puerto Rican who knew how to relate to and influence mainland US audiences due to my experience as a businessman. My skills were not technical. I was simply a good salesman (and a good recruiter and manager of other salespeople). I agreed to take the job because I believed in the group's objective: achieving self-determination for Puerto Rico through decolonization.

When I spoke to members of Congress, I targeted my message from the mainland US perspective. I tried to get them to see how a change in Puerto Rico's political status would bring fairness to the island's relationship with America and empower a disenfranchised population of American citizens. I explained how the United States government has consistently refused to give the Puerto Rican people what they really need to prosper: sovereignty, for which they have been waiting for more than 500 years. Unfortunately, some members of Congress would have the nerve to tell me that Puerto Ricans have shown through other referendums that they simply can't decide on what they want. They would say this even though numerous Supreme Court decisions have specifically ruled that Puerto Ricans have no right to self-determination and only the US Congress can decide the territory's political status.

During my time lobbying Congress, I wrote a booklet entitled Puerto Rico at the Crossroads, which I circulated to many influential politicians. In it, I laid out in very technical terms all of the reasons why Puerto Rico's colonial status needed to change in order to secure the island's future. I've included an updated version of this booklet in the appendix, as much of what I wrote then remains surprisingly relevant. The crux of my argument was to make an informed decision, any colonized people need to have a mechanism to make that decision. Without sovereignty, either as voting citizens of the United States or as an independent nation of their own, there are just too many financial and political ingrained interests that prevent Puerto Ricans from deciding what is best. If Congress were to take away the tax credits and put US corporations on an even playing field with their counterparts both in Puerto Rico and the mainland US, only then would the people of Puerto Rico be free to make a choice about their political status. Unfortunately, my arguments never broke through. In 1998, the US House of Representatives passed a bill by one vote to create a framework for the people of Puerto Rico to hold a binding referendum on statehood, but the legislation died in the US Senate.

Today, Puerto Rico is once again at a crossroads. Since 1998, there have been several high-profile efforts at statehood, both in Puerto Rico and in the US Congress, but none have resulted in any decisive action. Certainly, there is more than one reason why statehood efforts have failed, but I believe the main reason is that the effort's leadership have refused to consider the simple fact that if you want to sell somebody something, you have to present it in a way that benefits the buyer, not the seller. Logical, legal arguments only work in court cases. When it comes to influence and motivation, you must use emotion to entice the buyer. Only then can you use logic to justify the buyer's emotions and compel him or her to take action. That is Selling 101, but most Puerto Rican statehood efforts to this point have ignored this lesson completely.

During the 2020 election, about half of the voters of Puerto Rico did not choose statehood as their preferred political status. You can intellectualize these results with all kinds of obscure arguments that, perhaps, the Puerto Rican voters were "confused" and did not really mean to say what their ballots actually said. You can even argue about the exact percentages by a couple of points. Whichever way you choose to look at it, approximately half the people of Puerto Rico who voted in the 2020 election did not vote "yes" for statehood.

Some think that the 2020 US election might have opened up a new opportunity for statehood. With the Democrats keeping the House, narrowly winning the Senate, and taking back the White House, the new approach may be to use this majority to make Puerto Rico a state, along with Washington, DC, so that the Democrats would add another four seats in the Senate and another six seats in the House—assuming all the elected officials from these two new states become Democrats, which is likely.

On the surface it sounds simple and logical and—who knows—it might even work. But in addition to the fact that about half the

Puerto Ricans who live on the island did not vote in favor of statehood, this is what the pro-statehood camp is up against:

- The many Puerto Ricans who now live in the US and do not favor Puerto Rican statehood as well as their elected officials, who are mostly Democrats.
- All the corporations that operate in Puerto Rico and support the "non-statehood" parties. These corporations enjoy billions of dollars in tax credits as long as Puerto Rico does not become a state. They also contribute millions of dollars to the Democratic Party and use their contributions as a "Sword of Damocles" during election season.
- The thousands of transplanted former US residents who have moved to Puerto Rico in order to avoid paying federal capital gains taxes—to the tune of hundreds of millions of dollars.
- And of course, the most formidable opposition: the entire US Republican Party, which does not want more Democrats in the Congress.

All of these potential opponents have very convincing stories to tell, including: "How can you make Puerto Rico a state if half the people of Puerto Rico don't want statehood?"

In light of all this, the idea of selling the idea of Puerto Rico's statehood to opposing Republicans and half the residents of Puerto Rico seems like a very heavy lift indeed. And since the main backers of the plan are US Congressional Democrats of Puerto Rican descent, there is a good chance that no matter how many Democrats vote for statehood in the Senate, there may be just enough Democrats supporting the Republicans to prevent statehood—especially since many statehood supporters are Republicans who campaigned for Donald Trump in Florida. This includes the newly elected, second-term resident commissioner from Puerto Rico, Representative Jennifer González. Will she be a loyal statehooder or a loyal Republican? And how about the other former government and administration officers—both elected and appointed—of the *Partido Nuevo Progresista* (PNP), which supports statehood and both Republicans who spent their time campaigning for Donald Trump, a president who indicated on many occasions his opposition to statehood for Puerto Rico. Which loyalty will they respond to?

When I went to Washington in the 1990s, I wanted statehood for Puerto Rico because I believed it was the best option for de-colonization—especially from an economic perspective. But with half the people of Puerto Rico opposed to statehood, I'm finding it difficult to continue supporting this solution. If even two-thirds of the people of Puerto Rico were to show a clear desire for statehood, then I would support their efforts. But if a clear majority of Puerto Ricans vote for a different political status, then so be it. I will support the will of Puerto Rico's people.

What I absolutely cannot support is Puerto Rico's abysmal status quo.

Over 50 percent of Puerto Ricans are below the official poverty line as measured by the US Central Bank. Puerto Rico's per capita income is less than half of the per capita income of Mississippi, which is the lowest per capita income state in the US. The total dollar amount of food stamps paid out to Puerto Ricans—they are paid in cash—is higher than any state in US. Making things worse, Puerto Rico must buy everything from the mainland US, and it must ship those goods using US flagships, which makes the cost of those goods much more expensive.

Puerto Rico's government is totally dependent on US transfer payments, which are today well over $10 billion per year and may be close to 50 percent of the island's current fiscal budget.

The island's total employment base has been as high as one million, but over the last ten years it has shrunk to around 900,000. About one-third of Puerto Rico's jobs come from government po-sitions, 8 percent from manufacturing, and 3 percent from US-controlled corporations, which often falsely claim to be the bedrock of the Puerto Rican economy. The rest is of the economy is driven by small local business—including retail, construction, finance, and services.

According to a 2020 Council on Foreign Relations report entitled, "Puerto Rico: A US Territory in Crisis," "annual economic growth fell by roughly 7.5 percent overall between 2004 and 2019, while Puerto Rico's population shrunk by more than 16 percent. It has also entered bankruptcy proceedings after defaulting on its massive debt, a downward spiral that has been compounded by natural disasters, government mismanagement and corruption, the coronavirus pandemic, and population decline."

I could go on, but I think I've made my point. This disaster is the result of hundreds of years of bad policy, unfair rules, turning a blind eye, and treating Puerto Rico as a "possession" rather a valued strategic partner in the Caribbean. Now, the US's neglect of its relationship with the island could come back to bite us in a big way. Would anyone be surprised if Puerto Ricans decided their relationship with America was toxic and voted against statehood? And would anyone be shocked if Puerto Rico looked elsewhere for a more attentive strategic partner—like China? I don't think so.

A PEOPLE'S HISTORY
OF PUERTO RICO

TO UNDERSTAND WHAT THE PUERTO RICAN PEOPLE MIGHT WANT TO-day, it's helpful to know about their history. Puerto Rico was discovered in 1493 by Christopher Columbus, who claimed it for the kingdom of Spain. The island's first official governor was Juan Ponce de Leon, a conquistador who is probably most famous for his brutal repression of the indigenous Taíno people. Puerto Rico remained a colony of Spain until 1897, when it was granted limited independence. Unfortunately, independence didn't last long. Toward the end of the Spanish-American War, Spain decided it wanted to sell its colonies to America for $20 million dollars. The US Congress rejected the offer and said Puerto Rico, Cuba, Guam, and the Philippines combined were not worth that much money. The sensationalist newspaper magnate William Randolph Hearst—who had whipped up public sentiment for the Spanish-American War in the first place—offered to buy the four colonies outright. Congress, however, did not think it would be appropriate for a private individual to own four countries and Hearst was blocked from proceeding.

It seemed like all of the territories might be headed for independence until the US textbook lobby convinced Congress that if America bought the colonies, the US could impose English as the language of instruction in their schools. All four countries would then have to buy textbooks in English, which of course would be produced in America. This way, the textbook lobbyists argued, the $20 million investment (plus profit) would be recovered by the US. Unfortunately, someone forgot to tell the US Congress that Spain had no right to sell Puerto Rico, which had been on the road to independence since 1897—no matter, we all know money talks. The US purchase of Puerto Rico was completed on October 18, 1898, and US troops quickly occupied Puerto Rico as their bought and paid for "possession."

In the early days, there was a lot of anti-American activity—insurrections, protests, and other guerrilla conflicts. The US was dealing with similar conflicts in the Philippines and Cuba, giving Cuba its independence four years later in 1902. Then, in 1916, Congress passed a bill called the Jones Act that granted independence to the Philippines, though it wouldn't be completed until the end of the Second World War thirty years later. After losing Cuba and the Philippines, America did not want to give away Puerto Rico, so it devised an interesting "trick" in order to stop the insurrections, which were costing the US much in blood and treasure. By "trick," I'm referring to the chess term where no matter what move you make, you lose. It was simple: Congress passed the second Jones Act to make Puerto Ricans US citizens in 1917 (see the appendix at the back of the book for the text of this and other US laws passed about Puerto Rico). This bill was primarily aimed at regulating US shipping, but as an afterthought, the drafters added a couple of pages granting Puerto Ricans US citizenship.

There was plenty of furor about this decision in the US Congress. Formal hearings devolved into shouting matches about how Puerto

Rican "mongrels" could not possibly be made US citizens when they weren't even real humans like true Americans. Even President Woodrow Wilson was quoted as making such statements. Amid the din, Congress settled on the idea of giving Puerto Ricans "temporary" or statutory US citizenship. This way, Congress could revoke their citizenship status at any time. This is effectively the moment when Puerto Ricans became second-class citizens—quite a "trick," hey?

The second Jones Act also gave the US government the ammunition to put into prison anyone who spoke or acted against US interests. By making Puerto Ricans US citizens, insurrectionists were no longer legally considered "freedom fighters." Not only did this mean no more outside support, but it also meant they were now considered terrorists and could be charged with sedition and executed or imprisoned for life. None of this was fair, but back then who cared? After all, the people of Puerto Rico were just "mongrels" who did not deserve the same freedom of expression or peaceful assembly that "real" American citizens on the mainland enjoyed.

Make no mistake about it, the US knew exactly what it was doing. While most imperialist nations during that time had battled insurrections among their colonies, Puerto Rico had only one minor insurrection in its entire colonial history—and it was well before US colonization: the *Grito de Lares*, which translates into English as Cry of Lares. The revolt began in 1868 after a Jewish shoe manufacturer from New Orleans moved his factory to Lares, Puerto Rico, where labor was cheaper than on the mainland US. This sounds a lot like what US manufacturers have been doing over the last couple of decades by moving to Mexico or China, doesn't it? Well, sometime after this move, Spain decided to put a special tax on leather goods, which affected the shoe manufacturer's profits. He was faced with a decision: either close his factory and put his workers out of a job or demonstrate against the tax. He chose the latter, telling his workers to march with him, protest the tax, and demand independence from Spain. The protesters were quickly put down. Given this relatively passive history, the US must have thought Puerto Ricans would not seriously push for independence if a roadblock like "US citizenship" was placed in front of them. And guess what, US policymakers were right. To this day, Puerto Rico is the only colony in the history of colonialism that has never mounted a successful insurrection against its colonizers.

Another important factor that molded Puerto Rico's economic and cultural development was its connection to the Louisiana Territory, which was briefly ruled by Spain following France's defeat in the Seven Years War. The problem with both Louisiana and Puerto Rico was that estate distribution was governed by French colonial codes. Basically, this meant that if you had one hundred acres and fifty slaves to work the land, your ten kids would each inherit ten acres and five slaves. This was called "forced heirship," and still exists in a watered-down form in both Louisiana and Puerto Rico today.

Most Spanish colonies in the Caribbean were populated by Spaniards along with the slaves and descendants. An Irish-born military reformer named Alejandro O'Reilly changed that. He was sent to Louisiana by Spain in 1769 to implement land reform. Here is how he did it: He spread the word that if anyone in Europe brought 125 slaves from Africa to Louisiana or Puerto Rico, that person would be granted up to one thousand acres of land. O'Reilly's reforms encouraged Germans to come to Puerto Rico to raise pigs in Utuado; Corsicans to come and grow coffee in Yauco; the French to come and grow sugar cane in Guayama; among others. This is how Puerto Rico, unlike other Spanish colonies, became a multinational, multiethnic European society. Most of the native inhabitants were killed off within a few short years by the colonizers and the diseases they brought from Europe.

After the island's acquisition by America, local politics were essentially nonexistent. Between 1898 and the late 1940s the governor of Puerto Rico was always appointed by the president of the United States. But things began to change in the Cold War era. In 1948, the first elected governor of Puerto Rico was installed in *La*

Fortaleza (The Fortress), which is the governor's mansion. His name was Luis Muñoz Marín, and his impact on Puerto Rican politics cannot be overstated.

Mr. Muñoz Marín was a brilliant guy. The son of Luis Muñoz Rivera, who was the resident commissioner in Washington, DC, Muñoz Marín spent some time in Greenwich Village, New York, writing for one of the local newspapers there in the 1930s and early 40s. This was the age of the "beatniks," and Muñoz Marín was known to hang out with other writers, artists, musicians, revolutionaries, and intellectuals like himself. Some accounts paint him as an opium addict, but this may have been a politically motivated attack based on his often slovenly appearance. Being the son of the Puerto Rico resident commissioner in Washington DC, Muñoz Marín was closely surveilled by the FBI for most of his life. If you want to learn more about Mr. Marín, the book, *War Against All Puerto Ricans,* by Nelson A. Denis contains all the FBI files on him. As a result of those files, however, the White House was able to control Puerto Rico's first elected governor.

Muñoz Marín brilliantly promoted his agenda, wooing the press and using them to strengthen his position as governor. My neighbor and friend, Ronald Walker, a journalist in Puerto Rico, used to tell me how Muñoz Marín would invite every member of the press to his house on Sundays for hamburgers and beer. No, the governor didn't serve them local *arroz con pollo, carne frita, tostones* or *asopao* with drinks like *cañita* or *pitorro.* Instead, Muñoz Marín personally grilled hamburgers and poured mugs of beer, both of which he knew the press corps would love. This display of humility, in my opinion, can give leaders immense power because it builds loyalty—and Muñoz Marín was a master at this.

Early in his career, Governor Muñoz Marín's primary goal was to establish a special political status for Puerto Rico as a true "commonwealth." In other words, he wanted a political status for Puerto Rico that would contain elements of sovereignty with a close relationship with the United States. Today, most Puerto Ricans call this "free association" status. But Muñoz Marín did not get what he wanted from the US Congress. Public Law 600, which was passed in 1950, invited Puerto Rico to draft a constitution. Puerto Rico approved Congress' offer in a referendum on June 4, 1951, and the island's constitutional convention was held from September 1951 to February 1952. A few months later, on March 3, 1952, Puerto Ricans approved the constitution in a referendum and sent it to President Harry Truman, who in turn sent it to Congress for approval. With the passage of Public Law 447 in 1952, Congress conditionally approved the new constitution and Puerto Rico accepted Congress' requested changes. Puerto Rico's status as a commonwealth was proclaimed on July 25, 1952. This guaranteed the people of Puerto Rico only "limited self-government." Muñoz Marín told Congress this was insufficient, that Puerto Rico was still being treated as a colony under the new law. The Governor promised Congress he would put the issue to a vote in Puerto Rico. If the people of Puerto Rico rejected limited self-government, he told US lawmakers, he would be back for the real thing—sovereignty. But when the governor arrived back to Puerto Rico, he told the people that the US Congress had given them a new status that he called a "free associated state," in Spanish *estado libre asociado*. In an overly confident gesture, he implied that Puerto Rico was no longer a colony of the US. Secretly, Muñoz Marín was sure that when Senator John F. Kennedy became president, Puerto Rico would finally get the "free associated state" status he had long sought, as this was what the Senator from Massachusetts had promised. So, the myth continued, with Governor Muñoz Marín relying on Senator Kennedy's promise and members of Muñoz Marín's political party, the Popular Democratic Party (PDP), believing in President Kennedy's unfulfilled promise to the people of Puerto Rico.

When Kennedy did become president some five years later, Muñoz Marín went to the White House to finalize the details. But Kennedy refused to see him. After waiting in the reception room for days, the governor packed his bags and went back to Puerto Rico brokenhearted. Read *The Disenchanted Island* by Ronald Fernandez if you want the whole story. A few years later, Muñoz Marín would quit politics and retire, thoroughly disappointed at the treatment that he'd received from the White House. His successor, Roberto Sánchez Vilella became Puerto Rico's next governor, even as Muñoz Marín's myth of a "free associated state" lived on. You see, Muñoz Marín never fully communicated to the people of Puerto Rico that he had not been able to deliver on his promise—leaving many on the island believing they no longer lived in a colony when in fact they did.

I asked a good friend of mine, José Alfredo Hernández Mayoral, for his thoughts on Muñoz Marín's legacy. "Muñoz Marín led and governed according to clearly defined social goals, which he often outlined in public," he told me. My friend then quoted an interview with Muñoz Marín from the 1945 book, *Dynamite at our Doorstep*. At the time Muñoz Marín was president of the Puerto Rican Senate and was asked what he thought were the reasonable requirements of life. He answered:

> First of all, something that is defined by the Greeks as sincerity [note: Hernandez believes this was a mistranslation of "serenity"]—then sunlight, gardens, peace of mind, love of your children, time for thinking about God, and all other things that are good and great and free and don't require exploitation or taking anything from anyone else. You should have a roof over your head, good relations with your family. You should have honest relations with the human beings whom you contact in life–no fear of hunger or insecurity. You should do as many creative things as you can.

In a speech a decade later, Muñoz Marín expanded on many of those thoughts:

> That our people will live each day increasingly achieving their heart's desire: a solid middle-class life, not a life in the

shanties. That they have the opportunity to do honorable work at an adequate wage and live a good, peaceful life. This is at the heart of the people's dream for our nation.

That families will gain confidence from educating their children, thereby preparing them for the future and protecting them from illness, old age, and bad luck. This is at the heart of the people's dream for our nation.

That those willing to work hard will gain something more in this life, perhaps much more, but that no one will have less. This is at the heart of the people's dream for our nation.

That people will be able to work with pleasure, with freedom, with duty, with their rights protected, and with respect for one another. That people will contribute to the general good and see this as a positive opportunity, not just a duty. This is at the heart of the people's dream for our nation.

Muñoz Marín's heart was likely in the right place, but America did not give him an opportunity to deliver on his promise. He wanted Puerto Rico to be recognized as a true nation with a close relationship with the US, not merely as a "possession" owned by an occupier. In his last State of the Commonwealth Address in 1964, Muñoz Marín enumerated what he called the "Purpose of Puerto Rico."

Quality education and access to health care must be available to all and contribute to our nation's wellbeing.

Each family should be able to own their own home and the development of our country should be equitable between rural and urban areas. The wealth created by the growing Puerto Rican economy must benefit all, and consequently the private sector should leave a better world for our country's children and abolish extreme poverty forever.

I salute Muñoz Marín for his ideals! And I can't really blame him for not being completely clear about Puerto Rico's status because I believe he really expected Senator Kennedy to deliver on his promise when he became president. Welcome to politics! I once heard a comedian say all politicians make the same solemn promise: "If elected, I promise that all my promises will always remain promises." Unfortunately, Governor Muñoz Marín fell for it. But I still think he was brilliant. Here's one more reason why: In 1954, 50 percent of Puerto Ricans did not have shoes. Puerto Rico had the lowest per capita income in the Caribbean. People lived in thatched huts with dirt floors and worked for starvation wages that the plantations, farmers, and other business owners paid them in the form of credits that could be used to buy things at the "company store." The whole thing was rigged against the poor. Muñoz Marín wanted to change that, so he promoted what he called "Operation Bootstrap," bringing US manufacturing to Puerto Rico. Within one generation, Puerto Ricans were living in new Levittown homes, driving Toyotas, and wearing new shoes.

PUERTO RICO VERSUS HAWAII

Hawaii was often cited to demonstrate the expectation that if Puerto Rico became a US state, it would lead to more profitable local businesses and a healthier economy for the Caribbean island. In 1960, the year Hawaii became the fiftieth US state, both Puerto Rico and Hawaii had about ten thousand hotel rooms. Today, Hawaii has more than one hundred thousand while Puerto Rico still has around ten thousand. All you have to do is walk through the main tourist areas of each island to see the stark contrast of these two economies. While Hawaii's economy has expanded significantly since the 1960s, Puerto Rico's economy has stalled, and its territorial status is not helping.

With China moving into the Caribbean, the smart move for America would be to swiftly make Puerto Rico the fifty-first state, just like it did to Oklahoma, Alaska, and Hawaii—and for similar reasons. The people of those territories were not given the chance to exercise "self-determination" privileges because they didn't have them—just like Puerto Rico does not have them. These territories never "chose" statehood; Congress simply made them states because it was in America's best interest. Of course, times have changed. Puerto Rico will play a role in determining its future status, and statehood might not end up being the choice. However, there is a clear history of economic success demonstrated by Hawaii that Congress and Puerto Ricans should study as part of their decision-making process.

In the long run, "Operation Bootstrap" was both a miracle and a curse. While it quickly brought Puerto Rico's economy out of the dark ages and into the modern world, it also established US corporations as the principal arbiters of both Puerto Rico's political status and its economy. To this day, these corporations still call the shots when it comes to Puerto Rico's status both in local government and in US Congress. These companies spend millions lobbying both groups to get what they want, and their interests are not always aligned with those of the Puerto Rican people. My friend José Alfredo perhaps sums up Muñoz Marín best:

> He was consistent in his thoughts and priorities, and his achievements in those areas were remarkable. When he started, 70 percent of the population had never seen a doctor. When he left office, life expectancy had risen by twenty years. The economic miracle needs no retelling, nor the gradual elimination of slums [. . .] *Independentistas* hate Muñoz because he abandoned independence and created the commonwealth concept. And so, they accuse him of bending over to the US, even of being the victim of blackmail by the US (with no proof besides a Hoover file as credible as his other files). But that switch was very much in line with how he prioritized. People need shelter, education, good health, more than they need 'sovereignty.' And, more than any other Puerto Rican before him or since, he gave them that.

In the late 1960s, Governor Muñoz Marín's successor, Mr. Sanchez Vilella, was defeated by the wealthiest man in Puerto Rico, Luis A. Ferré, who formed the PNP. The party explicitly advocated for statehood, which I believe Ferré only supported in order to be able to control the process so that Puerto Rico would never actually become a state. His net worth was rumored to be in the hundreds of millions. In those days, if Puerto Rico became a state, half of his wealth would have gone to the federal government when he died. His heirs didn't like that, so they used one of the "family businesses," a powerful news media empire, to promote an opposition to statehood. With a suspect smile, he just looked the other way.

Puerto Rico now has three main political parties aligned along political status positions: PNP, which favors statehood; Partido Democratico Puertoriqueño (PDP), which favors maintaining the current colonial status; and the Partido Independentista Puertoriqueño (PIP), which favors independence. The PIP consists of true blue nationalist *independentistas* who just want pure independence for Puerto Rico, with no "free association agreement." They usually pull around 5 percent of the vote.

The PDP, however, is split between those that would prefer a "free association agreement" as a sovereign nation with the US who represent better than 50 percent of their voters. The PDP is mainly backed by the US-controlled foreign corporations who spend many millions of dollars to prevent statehood for Puerto Rico because they would have to pay federal taxes and would lose billions in federal tax credits. They fully support the PDP and spend many more millions lobbying US Congress and giving political contributions to them to make sure statehood does not happen.

The PNP, even though they claim to prefer statehood, know that when statehood is achieved, they will be "out of business" as a party and have to choose whether to align with Republicans or Democrats. Many wealthy PNP members say they favor statehood but could turn against the idea if it appears that it might become a reality. Truth is, most don't want to pay federal taxes or lose their influence within the PNP party. The PNP is mainly financially supported by wealthy Puerto Ricans who want to maintain a close working relationship with government administrations, as is the case with businesspeople all over the world. However, the biggest voting bloc in the PNP is not wealthy—in fact, many are food-stamp recipients and live below the poverty line. Their interest in statehood is around the many federal benefits available to mainland US residents, but not Puerto Ricans. A former PNP governor, who served two terms as governor and two terms as resident commissioner, once declared: "Statehood is for the poor."

Some years ago in Puerto Rico, the sentiment toward statehood ran much higher. In those days, a pro-statehood governor could usually count on close to 50 percent of the vote in any given election. The last PNP governor that got elected, however, only got 41 percent of the vote. This indicates that sentiment toward statehood may be declining (see the chart in the appendix on past elections). In the 2020 election, the PNP pro-statehood governor won with only 32 percent of the vote, which means that currently about 68 percent of Puerto Ricans do not want a statehood governor and reject the statehood party.

Part of the reason for the move away from statehood and toward independence is because America has been dillydallying over the issue for too many years—dangling promises that it has failed to keep and creating roadblocks to prevent a change in Puerto Rico's political status. The sentiment that "America does not want us" is prevalent in Puerto Rico today. When intelligent people come to the realization that they are "not wanted," they usually search for a place where they are wanted. In my opinion, that is where Puerto Rico is headed today.

About ten years ago, the population of Puerto Rico was close to four million. But many statehooders tired of waiting for broken promises to materialize and instead moved to the I-4 corridor in Florida, which now has around 1.3 million Puerto Ricans living there. Mostly Democrats, they will vote for anyone who promises statehood for Puerto Rico. As voters go, they are quite the catch— their voting participation, educational background, and economic position are much higher than the rest of the population in the I-4 corridor. The exodus to Florida and a few other states continued in 2017, after Hurricane Maria devastated the island. By some estimates, close to five thousand residents died. President Donald Trump visited in the aftermath and started throwing toilet paper and paper towels at the crowd of residents who came to greet him. Today, there are barely three million residents left. Yes, your math is correct, nearly a quarter of Puerto Rico's population has left in the last decade. And many of the people who stayed would prefer a status other than statehood. The Chinese are paying close attention to this trend.

As a result of the exodus of one million Puerto Ricans—partially because of statehood and partially because of Hurricane Maria—there are now more than two hundred thousand abandoned homes in Puerto Rico. Would it not make sense to have a Puerto Rico Land Run like the one in Oklahoma some one hundred years ago? Any US citizen currently living on the mainland US could come and pick up his or her "house in paradise" absolutely free, as long as they were willing to renovate. By adding two hundred thousand additional mainland US voters to Puerto Rico, the next statehood referendum would likely bring in a clear majority—just like it did in Oklahoma. It's just an idea, but one thing is clear: Puerto Rico is in desperate need of new ideas from the people who have the most influence on its future—Americans. The political status of Puerto Rico is fully dependent on the influence created by the US and those who would profit from any of the three status options.

There is an old Chinese story about Confucius and a young man who thought he could fool the wise, old philosopher. The young man held a bird behind his back and asked Confucius if the bird was alive or dead. If Confucius said the bird was alive, the young man knew he could simply squash the bird and prove Confucius wrong. But the old man was indeed wise, and simply told the young man, "The bird is in your hands."

Yes, America, Puerto Rico is in your hands. The important question is: What will you do with it?

DECODING PUERTO RICO'S PURSE STRINGS

IF HISTORY IS ANY GUIDE, AMERICA SEES PUERTO RICO MORE AS A tax shelter than a US state or sovereign country. I know this because many wealthy Americans have told me this. It has also been in the news. In February 2021, when YouTube influencer, Logan Paul, told his twenty million podcast followers that he was moving from Los Angeles to Puerto Rico for the lifestyle and the island's tax breaks, a *Time* magazine article appeared, entitled "How Puerto Ricans Are Fighting Back Against the Outsiders Using the Island as a Tax Haven." The article spoke of islanders "fed-up with the influx of rich mainlanders" seeking to shelter their incomes from taxation by moving to the Caribbean Island.

Tax laws can be tricky in any country, but they have been a political minefield during the sovereignty debate in Puerto Rico. It took me a very long time to figure out that wealthy Puerto Ricans may not support statehood as they claim, even as they donate to pro-statehood organizations. Their feelings for statehood may be genuine, but its implementation causes, what I might call, "a situational conflict with self-interest." Over and over again, these wealthy Puerto Ricans "talk the talk," but won't "walk the walk." Why? Tax laws—plain and simple. You see, those with the most clout on the island have the most to lose when tax laws change under US statehood. But I didn't understand this for many years. Once again, a series of seemingly random life events would lead me to important "ah, ha" moments that would enrich my understanding of Puerto Rico's complex political, social, and economic tapestry and how it impacts the island's sovereignty debate.

By the late 1980s and early 1990s, my life was beginning to settle into a new routine. Having sold out my insurance and securities operations to Aetna in 1985, I finally had the freedom to restructure my professional and personal life without the shackles of a business to manage. I spent my winters at my home in Colorado, running a Vail ski school program called "From Ski Tips to Stock Tips" (see the brochure in the appendix) and writing a financial column for Scripps Howard. I even managed to author another book called *$ . . . Making It and Keeping It!* and publish a newsletter called *Money Mastery*. In the summers, I could either be found skiing in South America or spending time in Europe with my family members who still lived there. Life was wonderful!

It was around this time that a good friend, the brilliant Ms. Inez Stewart, introduced me to an attorney named Manuel Rodríguez Orellana. At the time, he was a tenured professor of international law at Northeastern University in Boston. When Senate hearings began on Puerto Rico status in 1990, chaired by Senator J. Bennett Johnston of Louisiana, Manuel was invited as a member of the leadership of the PIP, the Puerto Rico Independence Party in English. He resigned his professorship and flew back to Puerto Rico to devote his attention to this process full time.

One day, Manuel said to me, "Alex, you have been a businessman in Puerto Rico now for almost twenty years. How do you feel about living in a colony?"

I shrugged. I'd never given the issue much thought, but I could sense Manuel's concern. He invited me for a weekend celebration of the famous *Grito de Lares*, mentioned earlier in the book. There, I met people who really impressed me. Intellectuals like Rubén Berríos, Fernando Martín, and others helped me understand the underlying issues that were driving Puerto Rico's politics and the havoc colonial status was wreaking on the island's economy and identity. As reflected in the famous Broadway musical *West Side Story*, Puerto Rican culture was slowly being eroded by outside interests.

After my sixty years of exposure to Puerto Rico's distinct culture—which is different from that of other Spanish colonies for reasons previously described—I had grown to care deeply about these gentle people who are so culturally, intellectually, and racially diverse. I admired what I would describe as their "subtlety," which had developed over five hundred years of colonization. Some ridicule this as a "colonialist mentality," but to me it is a useful skill they have developed to help them survive hundreds of years under the yoke of one nation or another.

I decided it was time for Puerto Ricans to begin to celebrate their culture either as a US state—like the culturally unique states of Louisiana or New Mexico—or as an independent nation. Having been denied participation in American government for more than 120 years, Puerto Rico finally deserved self-determination. It was time.

When I finally realized where Puerto Rico was and where it might be going, I told Manuel, "I agree with you. This colonial status needs to end. But if Puerto Rico is completely cut off from the economic benefits it receives from the US, the next couple of generations could be devastated economically. And the worst part is that Puerto Rico might never catch up, and perhaps become another Haiti. Less disruptive than independence, might be sovereignty through statehood."

Manuel's response was, "Any kind of sovereignty is better than being a colony. Go for it!" Then he added, "Do you mind if I call you a lightly rooted nationalist?" We both laughed, and the label stuck. He still calls me this today.

Even though I had sold my insurance company and was traveling for much of the year, I still managed a personal finance consulting practice in Puerto Rico. My clients were small business owners and professionals with interest in creating capital and investing it wisely to achieve financial independence—as I had successfully done. I also had a couple of major clients for whom I did corporate work—crafting executive compensation and fringe benefits programs, managing some M&A activity, overseeing my investment, and offering others advice on how to do the same. But most of my clients came from US-controlled foreign corporations—CFCs, as I call them—that operated in Puerto Rico under Section 936 of the US Internal Revenue Code. I contracted with many of these companies to assist their local managers in Puerto Rico and their stateside executives with personal financial planning, a service offered by their employers as a fringe benefit.

Under Section 936, American corporations could funnel their Puerto Rico profits through their Puerto Rico subsidiary, then repatriate those profits tax-free to their parent companies. When Section 936 was eventually phased out over a ten-year period beginning in 1996, these companies could no longer repatriate profits tax-free, so they set themselves up as CFCs in order to remain tax exempt as far as the IRS was concerned. However, they could no longer send those profits back to their parent companies in the US anymore without paying taxes. Many of those companies then used their billions in tax-free revenue dollars to invest outside the US—and some of those profits even funded anti-statehood lobbying in Washington and Puerto Rico. But now, if they funneled all their worldwide profits through Puerto Rico shell companies, those profits would be tax free as long as they invested outside the US.

A conversation on a flight home after giving a personal finance seminar to a group of top executives at a major pharmaceutical in New Jersey opened my eyes and changed the course of my life. All of the pharma companies in attendance had operations in Puerto Rico, and I was seated next to one of the company's chief financial officers on the flight home. After a couple of drinks, our conversation got pretty loose.

"With IRC 936, you guys have a great deal," I said, sipping my drink. "You put together all your worldwide profits and funnel them through your Puerto Rico subsidiary and back to your parent company, and you pay almost no federal or Puerto Rico taxes. I guess that's why you are in Puerto Rico, right?"

"Yes, we have a great tax dodge there, but that is not why we are really in Puerto Rico. We are there for the cheap wages."

"Cheap wages?" I asked. "But Puerto Rico has the US minimum wage. In fact, the cost of doing business on the island must be much higher than on the mainland US."

My client just shook his head. "No, you see, our Puerto Rico operation is not labor-intensive; it is a capital and skilled personnel enterprise. Puerto Rico has a top engineering school located in Mayagüez. We hire chemical and other engineers from there for less than half of what we would have to pay an engineer from the mainland US. Saves us millions. The tax break is great, but we would still be there without it."

"But your message to both the Puerto Rico government and the US Congress is always 'if you take away the tax credit, we'll leave Puerto Rico,'" I pushed.

"Well, who wants to give away a multibillion-dollar tax break if we can have both? A little white lie doesn't hurt!"

A lightbulb went off—so that was it: All those CFCs were in Puerto Rico promoting a "little white lie." They weren't really there for the IRC Section 936 tax breaks, they were there for affordable, highly educated talent.

I couldn't sleep that night. I spent hours buried up to my eyeballs in research about Section 936, the IRC code, and the CFCs that were taking advantage of it. That weekend I wrote the next issue of *Money Mastery* and called it, "Puerto Rico at the Crossroads." It addressed the very points made during my conversation with the pharmaceutical CEO on the airplane, along with some of my own research on the topic. Within days of the release of that newsletter, I got a call from the chief legal counsel of a local corporation. He wanted to meet and told me that the elimination of IRC Section 936 would be the focal point of the attempt at decolonization of Puerto Rico through statehood because the greatest opponents to statehood were those companies. By eliminating Section 936, these companies could redirect a portion of the billions of dollars of income to fighting statehood. Even a small percentage of their annual tax credits could amount to tens or even hundreds of millions of dollars that they could invest into local politics every year by supporting the PDP, whose interest was also in preventing statehood, along with the lobbyists in Washington that would be promoting the continuation of these tax credits.

Now I was excited!

During our next meeting, I told the legal counsel for our group of statehood supporters that I was in with both feet and whatever they wanted me to do to help eliminate IRC Section 936, I was ready. They could count on me. I began attending meetings where we began planning the strategy that we might use in order to eliminate this IRC Section 936 and begin the decolonization process for Puerto Rico. Soon, I was summoned to Washington, DC to attend congressional hearings related to Section 936. I was in Denver for ski season, and I remember abruptly canceling my lesson commitments to hop on the next plane to Washington.

The CFCs were caught unawares by our moves in Washington. As a result, we soon gained a ten-year phaseout of IRC Section 936. As they always did, the CFCs all threatened to leave Puerto Rico if the phaseout was actually implemented, but none of them did. In fact, most expanded their operations on the island. The phaseout of Section 936 was finally implemented. It was only the beginning of the decolonization process, but it was a big win for us (see the updated 1998 version of *Puerto Rico at the Crossroads* in this book's appendix for more about this issue). The natural next step was elimination of IRC Section 933, but nobody wanted to talk about that one.

Section 933 gives Puerto Rico tax autonomy from the US. If you and your corporation are residents on the island, then any income from a Puerto Rican source is not taxable for federal income tax purposes. If Section 933 could be eliminated, Puerto Ricans would start paying federal income and estate taxes. And since Puerto Rico is still a territory, that tax revenue would stay on the island. The net fiscal result for residents and the Puerto Rico government was about the same. Only one thing would change: tax collection would now be guided by federal rules, not Puerto Rican rules. The US Virgin Islands already had this program in place, so why not Puerto Rico, too? To answer this question, we have to decode Puerto Rico's tax code.

Tax Blues

Most local businesses—big and small—in Puerto Rico are considered "closely held," meaning more than 50 percent of the value of the company's outstanding stock is owned (either directly or indirectly) by five or fewer individuals. In Puerto Rico, closely held companies operate under a Napoleonic rule of "forced heirship." This means that children, grandchildren, and direct descendants of business owners are guaranteed some interest in the business equal in value to their inheritance. The US does not.

With "forced heirship," the heirs of the deceased continue to participate financially in the company's profits and have an opportunity to enhance their personal net worth if the business continues to be successful. For the remaining business owners, there is also a benefit: They are not forced to sell the company at a discount or liquidate in order to pay off the deceased owner's heirs. It's a win-win. Statehood for Puerto Rico would open the door for rewriting "forced heirship" distribution laws so that wealthy family businesses don't go bankrupt and leave their heirs penniless if Puerto Rico becomes a state. This would mirror the way "forced heirship" rules are handled in the state of Louisiana. As you can imagine, the handling of "forced heirship" rules are a big consideration in the debate around Puerto Rican statehood. That is why Puerto Rico must address this issue before it becomes a state, just as Louisiana did. Otherwise, no Puerto Rican business owner could possibly accept statehood, as it would mean the financial destruction of their extended family heirs.

Valuation Troubles

There is also a difference between how the US and Puerto Rico value business assets when it comes to estate taxes. Typically, estate taxes are paid in cash within a year of the time that the estate goes through probate. But even though the business may have a "going concern value" based on IRS calculations—this could be in the millions of dollars—its real market value might be much lower, especially after an owner dies. The problem is that in the US, the IRS values a business on the day *before* the owner died. This means that the business is valued on the income it was generating while it was still being successfully operated by the now-deceased principal. The IRS calls this the "going concern value," which could be many times higher than the "book value," which only appraisal existing depreciated assets. The difference between these two valuations can be substantial—and life altering.

Without "forced heirship," this valuation problem has plagued American businesses and their heirs for years, especially small farmers. Fortunately, the IRS raised the exemption on estate taxes to over $20 million so that smaller businesses will no longer be caught in a valuation trap. Let me demonstrate with a bit of an exaggeration. Suppose the "going concern value" of a business is $300 million but the book value (depreciated assets) is only worth $3 million with a corporate surplus of $2 million. This means we have a $5 million book value and a $300 million going concern value. That is a huge difference. The federal estate taxes on the "going concern value" would be $120 million (40 percent of the going concern value) while 40 percent of the book value would be only $1.2 million. If a business was producing a $30 million cash flow while the deceased principal was still alive, and those earnings plummet to $10 million upon his or her death, then value of that business in a sale for $100 million after selling costs, would leave four heirs, each able to pocket $25 million, but owing $30 million each to the IRS. One minute, multimillionaires, the next they're broke and $5 million in debt to the IRS with no income. This may be a simplistic example, and exaggerated, but the mechanics are mostly correct. The realities of the math make it difficult for statehooders with successful businesses to follow through without penalizing their heirs if statehood is successful.

These are a few reasons why when statehood for Puerto Rico looks like it might be possible, someone throws a wrench into the process and stops it. That someone is usually a local businessman who is well aware of the way federal estate taxes can destroy his or her family fortune. Most of the time, our roadblock would turn out to be an ardent "statehooder" in public, even as he or she worked behind the scenes to thwart our progress.

It's easy to get frustrated, but you have to ask yourself, if you were a wealthy Puerto Rican running a family business and whose financial wellbeing depended on paying no federal estate taxes upon your death, would you really welcome statehood in Puerto Rico before you died? I know I would be lying if I answered, "Yes."

Human nature dictates that self-interest take precedence over altruism. We only do "good stuff" if doing the "good stuff" helps us, not hurts us. In the words of Adam Smith, "it is not from the benevolence of the butcher, the brewer, or the baker that we expect our dinner, but from their regard to their own interest." Do I blame those wealthy Puerto Ricans for wanting to preserve their family wealth? Of course not. But after thirty years of pursuing statehood for Puerto Rico, getting so close, and then watching key players pull back, it's frustrating to hear members of the US Congress insist that Puerto Ricans simply don't know what they want. It would be much more accurate for Congress to assert that the average Puerto Rican is forced to choose between a rock and hard place—and that harsh environment was in good part created by America.

TAXES AND YOUR *PANA*

I have been audited by both the US federal government and the government of Puerto Rico. The two experiences could not be more dissimilar. In the US, the first thing to remember is to make sure that you report all your income on your tax returns. If you take a deduction, you must have a legal basis to justify that deduction. When your Internal Revenue Service (IRS) examining agent feels comfortable that you are not breaking the law, he or she will discuss with you or your accountant the "reasonableness" of your deduction and basis in law that it represents. In my experience, the IRS has been most helpful in working out issues—but only for those who have been fully forthcoming. It's a fairly predictable experience.

In Puerto Rico, I call the tax audit process, "¡Ay, *bendito*!" Loosely translated, this means something close to "Oh, dear!" It's an expression of worry and concern.

Here's how the process works: Your accountant meets with the tax examiner and goes through the ritual of discussing which family members and friends you might have in common and what personal interactions all involved parties might have had—the examiner, you, and your accountant. The purpose of this ritual is to determine whether your income tax examiner might be your *pana*. The term *pana* is confusing. In Spanish, it means breadfruit. But *pana*'s modern meaning emerged during the original American occupation of Puerto Rico in 1898. It appears that many of the occupying soldiers were from the southern US and called their friends "partners." When you pronounce "partner" with a southern accent, it sounds like *pana*. Overtime, *pana* became the person who took care of you when you needed help. Need a loan? Find your *pana* at the bank. Traffic violation? You need a police *pana*. Looking for a housing permit? Find a *pana* at the department of housing.

And, of course, when you are being audited, you need a *pana* at the *hacienda*—Puerto Rico's version of the IRS. That's why, while you and your accountant are talking small talk with your income tax examiner, you are always looking for common ground to establish that *pana* relationship. That conversation might look like:

"After a thorough examination," the tax examiner says, "we find that your client owes us $100,000."

"¡Ay, bendito! How did you come up with such a figure?" your accountant responds.

"Well, since your client is a prominent professional or businessman," the examiner continues, "we could make an exception and bring that down to $50,000."

"That sounds better," your accountant replies. "But, ¡ay, bendito! My client's mother is sick. He's not paying attention to the business. Profits are low and his medical expenses are high. Could we make it $5,000?"

"How about $10,000?" says your accountant's new *pana*.

"Deal," says your accountant. "Let's shake on it!"

Obviously, this is a gross exaggeration of Puerto Rico's tax audits. But it illustrates the difference between the island's personal approach and the strictly legal approach stateside.

Many "moneyed" Puerto Ricans are very reluctant to give up the island's "¡Ay, bendito!" approach. Without a *pana*, life would be a lot more complicated for most Puerto Ricans, especially the wealthy ones. This is one reason many rich Puerto Ricans don't want to switch to the US's federal IRS tax and audit system.

Another reason, a more important one, is that under the island's tax code, there are no "death taxes" on properties held in Puerto Rico. And if US properties are held in Puerto Rico LLCs, then those may be considered Puerto Rico properties as well. Today, under the IRS federal tax code, any amount over $20 million in an estate is taxed at 40 percent. A few years ago, any amount over $600,000 was taxed at 50 percent. Not many wealthy Puerto Ricans would want to give away half of their estate to the US federal government, which is what would happen if Puerto Rico became a state.

5

THE YOUNG BILL

IN 1998, I WORKED WITH MEMBERS OF THE US CONGRESS TO CREATE a framework for the people of Puerto Rico to have a referendum on statehood, using realistic political status definitions, which could result in a possible change of the current territorial status. If the people of Puerto Rico so desired, they could either become a state, declare their independence as a sovereign nation, or continue living as a colony.

That last option is more fraught with problems than it might seem at first glance. One of the problems that our group of statehood advocates found in sponsoring local referendums (called plebiscites) on Puerto Rico's status was that independence and statehood were very easy to define. For independence, you either have full sovereignty, or you don't. For statehood, you either have a star on the flag, or you don't. But for the word "commonwealth," which describes the current colonial/territorial status of Puerto Rico, the definition could be almost anything to voters.

My decision to enter national politics came at a serious financial cost. For one, I lost most of my CFC clients, which represented 50 percent or more of my consulting practice. They did not want someone working for them that was also working to eliminate their tax credits. I also lost many of my smaller clients because I could no longer give them the attention they needed. My consulting practice shrunk significantly. National politics thrust me into a world of infighting, campaign contributions and fundraisers, and deal making with members of Congress—in general, the nasty busy world of professional politics.

But all of that sacrifice would be worth it if we could get the law passed. It had the potential to change Puerto Rico forever. The referendum bill—called the Young Bill after sponsor Congressman Don Young of Alaska—included in its report the true definition of the current political status of the island. The House legal department specifically stated in its Young Bill report that Puerto Rico was an unincorporated territory, a possession, with no rights other than those that Congress gave it.

As proof of this statement, Congress subsequently imposed a board of directors on Puerto Rico that would report directly to Congress about key issues concerning Puerto Rico "self-government" so that Congress could decide how to properly address those decisions. If they disagreed, Congress claimed the right to impose their views on this American "colony" in any way it chose.

This board of directors was implemented with the recommendation of Pedro Pierluisi, a member of the PNP and the newly elected governor who had garnered only 32 percent of the vote. With that action, in my layman opinion, Mr. Pierluisi effectively eliminated the clause in the 1954 law that Puerto Rico was entitled to have "limited self-government." Now, the US Congress had the full power to make all the local decisions related to governing Puerto Rico.

But the most important result of the Young Bill effort was that the followers of Governor Muñoz Marín and the PDP party realized that they had been misled. They quickly began a movement to establish the status that Governor Muñoz Marín had originally intended to implement, which was a contract of free association with the US that included full sovereignty, like the Samoans and other islands in the Pacific have today.

Before the Young Bill, the issue of Puerto Rico independence was supported by less than 5 percent of the population because half the island believed that they already had status as *estado libre asociado,* or free associated state. Today, my guess is that at least one-third of Puerto Ricans are in favor of independence through a "free association contract." So, who should the *independentistas* thank for this heavy lift? Those of us who promoted the Young Bill. We believed Puerto Ricans really wanted statehood and that the Young Bill would pave the way for this event. We should have remembered the adage, though, to "beware of unintended consequences." They usually allow for the real truth to come out.

In order to really see that truth, however, you need to understand exactly what we were trying to accomplish with the Young Bill and the circumstances that led to its drafting. Before the Young Bill could even be submitted in the US Congress, those of us behind the scenes worked to secure a number of necessary assets:

- A local team that would develop the strategy and participate in fundraisers for members of Congress along with meetings on the Hill. People that could say: "I am from Puerto Rico, and I want to talk to you about a bill to help Puerto Rico with political self-determination."
- A vehicle with which to funnel the contributions for the "cause" and allocate and monitor expenses of promoting such legislation. This vehicle would be a 501(c)(4) organization, which was categorized as an "educational foundation." The donations were not tax deductible, but any profits were exempt from taxes.
- Expert consultants that would advise the "local team" as to the best way to approach Congress or the administration on issues dealing with the proposed legislation.

- Lobbyists in Washington, DC who would set up the appointments for members of the "local team" with members of Congress to promote our issue.
- Champions that were themselves members of Congress, but that would have a strong commitment to our cause and who would promote our message to their colleagues in Congress.
- Committed sources of contributions, which would come in two types. One would be funds to support the lobbying expenses and pay the consultants and other expenses related to the effort. The other would be sources of campaign donations to the members of Congress that were champions and cosponsors for various bills and resolutions that might be helping the effort.
- Members of the local Puerto Rico legislature and administration that would support our cause in Washington, DC.
- Polling experts that would keep us on the right track in terms of our messaging and monitoring the results of our promotion to see if we were making progress.
- Event managers, who were public relations people, who would set up events for us to promote our statehood issue with those who might be willing to help us.

If you add up the costs of all the above services and consider the elevated costs of doing business in Washington, DC, it is easy to see that such an effort took very deep pockets. With our group, I was close enough to the total cash outflow to have some idea as to what this expense might be. My best guesstimate ran in the millions per year.

Our core group of statehood advocates was around a dozen or so people who came from various backgrounds, but most of the participants were attorneys. As a longtime resident of Puerto Rico, I became a member of the "local" team. I will never forget the day we invited a prominent DC lobbyist to give us an orientation. He was an attorney and professor of public affairs at GWU. We were all complete neophytes on the workings of Washington, but we were eager to learn. So, we asked him, "How do we get to talk to members of Congress to tell them our story so we can get a bill in Congress to help us achieve statehood?"

The simplicity of his response surprised me. "First, you find some members of Congress that may want to support your cause. Then you give them a campaign contribution to get them interested. After that, you keep making those campaign contributions until your bill is passed."

Capitol Hill is fueled by money. It gobbles up dollars like a hungry hog. If you want something from Washington, you'd better be ready to open up your wallet. There are no "free lunches" there— and no friends. Everything is either "cash on the barrelhead," or go play somewhere else. As President Truman once said, "If you want a friend in Washington, get a dog." I was learning this lesson very quickly.

When we asked for more detail as to how we find these interested members of Congress, the lobbyist laid out the whole process in helpfully candid terms: "You identify someone you would want to talk to because he or she may have some connection or affinity to your cause. You offer them a 'campaign contribution' to smooth the way for the meeting. You tell them what you need from that member of Congress and ask them if they would be willing to support your cause. The member will talk to their campaign director and explain to them what you want, and the campaign director will evaluate to see if the member's involvement will help or hurt the member's next election. If it will hurt, the member's staffer will call you and tell you that his boss would prefer not to get involved. If the issue will help the election (or at least be neutral), the member's finance director will get back to you and tell you what the financial expectations might be for this involvement in general terms."

The point to remember is that, in most instances, the members play it pretty straight. They cannot guarantee that they will do what you ask after you make your fundraisers and contributions for them.

That is called "quid pro quo," and it's illegal. But in most instances, if the member becomes interested in your objective, they will help you promote your cause—especially if it might help their reelection.

It took a few years to build up the operation to where we had the support of the key people in both local government and US Congress and identified the people who would be our champions. One of my roles in this process was the development of "interested" members of Congress who could become cosponsors for the bill's introduction to the House and Senate.

At that time, I had a house in Vail, Colorado, which I would use to host members of Congress for cocktails or dinner when they held events in mountain resort areas. The events usually had a tight schedule. In the winter, the day would be skiing, snowshoeing, or snowmobiling. In the summer, there would be mountain biking, golfing, hiking, or river rafting. The "program" would usually last three or four nights, with one of those nights being a "free night" with no events scheduled.

For members of Congress, this was a vacation. They brought their wives, their kids, their parents, and their friends with them. Since the expense reimbursement for members of Congress for the events did not include the cost of private ski instructors (who were expensive), the members were usually either on their own or in official organized groups. I quickly spread the word around that I was a fully certified ski instructor in Vail and announced that I would ski with anyone who wanted to ski with me. I had more takers than I could handle, which gave me an opportunity to give them my "Puerto Rico" pitch in a relaxed, private, and casual setting. Most chair lift rides last around seven minutes. This was the best venue with a captive audience because nobody can get off a chairlift in the middle of the ride. I was also able to bypass lift lines because the lift operators knew me. I would take my guests through the "instructor" line.

The other event I managed to put to good use was the "free night." Since the "program" evening events only allowed spouses to participate, leaving the entourage of parents, children, and friends to fend for themselves, I made a rule that all members who would like to join me at my house for the "free" evening for dinner and drinks were welcome, and their parents, kids, and friends were all welcome too with no exception.

After those events in Vail, I had many doors open to me on the Hill. It was a productive experience for our cause leading up to the Young Bill and for years thereafter. Remember the bill passed the House by one vote, and I wouldn't be surprised if that deciding vote might have been cast by someone who sipped champagne by a stone fireplace at one of those "free" evenings at my house in Vail.

As I said earlier, what I have learned over the last thirty-five years as a writer and consultant in areas of finance, economics and politics is that most readers don't want facts and figures—those just put them to sleep. They just want a good personal story, and that is precisely what I am trying to accomplish here. So rather than belabor the merits of the Young Bill, let us cut straight to how the vote played out.

I clearly remember the day bill was going to be introduced. It was 1996, the middle of an election year. A small group of us stood outside the House chamber waiting to see the bill introduce to the full House of Representatives. Congressman Don Young from Alaska, after whom the bill was named, was with us, as was Congressman Dan Burton, who was one of our key legislative champions. I paced, trying to manage my nerves. There was a lot riding on this bill, but we were confident it would pass the House. We had the votes, and the timing was perfect. After the election, Senator Larry Craig would reintroduce the bill to the Senate. The House could then go through the reconciliation process in 1997 and 1998 and have legislation ready for President Bill Clinton's signature before the next election cycle. Finally, I thought as I paced, we would be on our way to self-determination in Puerto Rico.

We were only moments away from seeing the bill "dropped" on the House floor. The excitement was palpable. Then, one of my colleague's phones rang. We all turned and watched him turn white. He walked over to Congressman Young and Burton and whispered a message. They also turned white as sheets. They had put their careers on the line for this bill, facing rebuke from their fellow Republicans. What the hell was happening? The caller, whose name was not shared with us, had said "kill the bill." As we walked out of the hall in utter shock, both congressmen put a hand on my shoulder. "Don't worry Alex, next year we are going to shove this bill down their throats!"

Unfortunately, they would be wrong.

6

POSSESSIONS

IN THE APPENDIX OF THIS BOOK, YOU WILL FIND AN UPDATED VERSION of my booklet, *Puerto Rico at the Crossroads*. Originally published in 1998, it will give you a shortened version of what happened with the Young Bill. If you want more detail of our statehood initiative, check out my book *Pay to the Order of Puerto Rico*, which describes the process that led to the drafting of the Young Bill, the arguments that went on in both US Congress and in the press while it was being considered, and what happened in the aftermath of the Young Bill's failure. Or just do your own research. Then, you be the judge.

But for the purposes of this narrative, here's a brief summation of why our statehood effort died: In 1996, the timing had been perfect for the Young Bill to become law, but the vote was pulled at the last minute. By the fall of 1997, we did not have enough time to get the bill through the Senate before the 1998 election season. We brought it for a vote in the House anyway, and to the Republican leadership's surprise, it passed by a single vote. Unfortunately, once the 1998 election season passed, it was dead on arrival in the Senate.

When we hit a brick wall in the Senate, we knew that passing the Young Bill in the House was all that we would get for our trouble. If we estimated approximately five years of preparation to get the Young Bill introduced in the House, plus a couple of years going through the process in the House and the Senate, and another year or so exploring how we might be able to resurrect our failure, my very ballpark guess was that during those seven or eight years we spent many millions on this doomed enterprise—not to mention all the time and effort we put in as a team.

This reminds me of a comedian who once made a joke about sending his son to summer camp, which cost him $1,000 dollars. The kid came home with an ash tray that he made in "arts and crafts," so the comedian put the ashtray on the shelf and labeled it as his "$1,000 ash tray" for all to see. I still scratch my head when I think about our multimillion-dollar "ash tray" that we made in our "summer camp" in Washington, DC.

Because of the suddenness of the vote delay in 1996, we all suspected that the bill had been sabotaged. Presumably, it was someone with a lot of power who did not want Puerto Rico to become a state. My guess was that the person who sabotaged the bill had publicly supported it—maybe even financed our effort—but never expected it to pass. He or she then stopped the bill when it became clear that it had a chance of passing, so he could mount an opposition to it clandestinely to make sure it did not pass the following year. In Washington, you can never be quite sure who your supporter and saboteurs are. They can come from the most unlikely of places.

In the wake of our failure, I began to wonder who this saboteur could be. It would have to be someone with connections to the Republican Whip in the House since it was clear that the Whip had expected the bill to come close and lose instead of passing by one vote. Eventually, I found out who killed the bill. On September 24, 1997, a full-page ad ran in the *Washington Times* by an organization called "Puerto Rico First." It talked about the "evils" of the Young

Bill (see the booklet in my appendix for more details). Its title, referring to the Young Bill's official designation, was "H.R. 856, the Budget Buster." Many other ads soon followed, run by this same organization. These ads were not complimentary of Puerto Ricans and used terms I would be embarrassed to describe or show you in this book. Appalled by the campaign, I decided to root out the financier of "Puerto Rico First." My research showed that the organization's headquarters were located in a very poor section of the San Juan metro area called Barrio Obrero, and its executive director was a Mr. Deposada, who was an unemployed truck driver. The attorney that set up the organization and filed it with the Department of State was a friend of mine, and so I asked him to have lunch.

During the lunch I asked him, "How could you represent an organization that would run ads like that, disparaging Puerto Ricans in general and the Young Bill specifically? I know that you are an avid supporter of Puerto Rico's statehood."

"Yes, Alex, I am a statehooder, but a very important client asked me to do this. He is one of the wealthiest people in Puerto Rico. So, unless I was willing to lose a client, I just did what he told me to do."

"You know," I smiled, "I probably would have done the same."

BOOM AND BUST IN PUERTO RICO

There are passages in *America's Last Fortress* that suggest that some wealthy Puerto Ricans have publicly supported a change of status for the island while privately opposing it—primarily due to possible changes in the law that would no longer protect their wealth from taxation. I am not alone in this observation. *Boom and Bust in Puerto Rico*, written by *San Juan Star* columnist Alex W. Maldonado, was released in August 2021. A former colleague of mine from my journalism days, Maldonado has written, what I believe to be, the best historical account of the formation of the Popular Democratic Party (PDP), or Commonwealth Party, which supports continuation of the island's current status.

Maldonado's book also covers the story of Governor Muñoz Marín's founding of the PDP and Luis A. Ferré's formation of the opposing New Progressive Party (PNP), which supports statehood—at least in theory. Back in the 1950s, Ferré was the wealthiest man on the island. From the start, Ferré publicly stated that commonwealth status should only be a stepping-stone to statehood. He got his start in politics in 1952 when he was elected to Puerto Rico's House of Representatives. In 1967, Ferré saw a chance to further his political career during the island's first plebiscite. Though the PDP's commonwealth option won out, Ferré utilized the plebiscite to mobilize statehood forces and establish a new political entity, the PNP. In 1968, Ferré ran for governor as the PNP candidate and won in a close race. His victory marked the end of 25 years of political dominance by the PDP. From that moment forward, the PNP and PDP would vie for the support of the Puerto Rican people.

What I have implied, and Maldonado has supported, is that when statehood got close to becoming a reality, Ferré and his people were quietly working against statehood while publicly campaigning for it. It's a bold claim, but I'm not the only one suggesting it. Here is an excerpt from Maldonado's book:

> When the New Progressive Party was organized...it left no doubt that it had a mission. Many of the young leaders had always expressed doubts about whether the Statehood Republican "old guard," the mixture of professional politicians who lived off their legislative salaries and reactionary businesspeople, were really committed to statehood. Some even doubted Ferré himself. Why would a wealthy Puerto Rican want to change to a status where he would have to pay full federal taxes? ...For many others, leaders and members of the Popular Democratic Party, it was not clear what would change. Ferré, after all, attempted to appeal to disaffected PDP, pro-commonwealth voters with his pledge that a vote for him was not a vote for statehood.

Though I don't agree with everything Maldonado says, his book is a must read for anyone interested in the development of Puerto Rico's political system and its impact on the island's economic progress.

That meeting convinced me that many wealthy Puerto Ricans talk statehood but oppose it behind the scenes. That's why they supported the Young Bill publicly but privately ensured its failure. To be fair, the Young Bill wasn't perfect. There were many legitimate reasons for it not to pass the US Congress—apart from nefarious backroom dealing. The official excuses for the opposition could be any of the following:

- Since those who voted in favor of the bill were mostly Democrats, Republicans perceived the Young Bill as a threat to the Republican Party's domination of Congress. The popular perception was that most Puerto Ricans were Democrats (which is true), and if Puerto Rico became a state, there would be five more Democratic members of the House and two more Democratic members of the Senate joining the US Congress.
- Puerto Rico's statehood would eliminate the tax credits that the CFCs had been enjoying, so their lobbying efforts with their unlimited resources outspent those in favor of statehood.
- The PDP party that was (and still is) against statehood because it is financially supported by the CFCs had Puerto Rican members of Congress who supported their anti-statehood position.
- Since the PDP party (favoring "commonwealth" status) combined with the PIP party (favoring independence) together represented about 50 percent of the votes in Puerto Rico, Congress felt that not enough Puerto Ricans wanted statehood to justify a process for that transition.

In my opinion, all of the above is absolutely true. But the real reason the effort failed, in my opinion, was the position of the wealthy Puerto Rico class. Most of them called themselves Republicans and were financially supporting our statehood efforts. Whenever we would get close; however, they would suddenly throw a wrench into the process. Why? Federal taxes!

As I referred to earlier in the book, some wealthy Puerto Rican families stood to lose upward of 50 percent of their family wealth upon the death of the key stockholder because of federal estate taxes. In some cases, losses could total as much as hundreds of millions of dollars. And since those taxes are paid in cash within a year of the probate of the estate, long-held family businesses might have to be sold at a discount in order to meet this tax obligation, which could wipe out the other 50 percent of the estate.

But the most glaring example of this position was when we had put together an argument (at considerable expense) to the IRS against a recently passed Puerto Rico Law 22, which allowed mainland US residents who took domicile in Puerto Rico to avoid paying federal taxes on US capital gains. This law created a natural opposition to statehood by those who took advantage of it.

Just before we launched a campaign in the US media to discredit this law, key contributors to our statehood cause suddenly told us to kill it. When I asked why, I was given some excuse that the circumstances were not quite right for the initiative at this moment and told to "file" the work that we had done on this issue, so we could revisit it later. As a result, thousands of hedge fund principals whose income was derived from federal capital gains taxes suddenly became part-time residents of Puerto Rico to avoid paying billions of dollars in taxes. Those same "Law 22" US residents, as they are called, are today the fiercest opponents to statehood; some are willing to spend millions of dollars to make sure that statehood does not happen.

As the former governor of Puerto Rico once said, statehood is for the poor, and the only thing that the poor have is their vote. But what really drives elections, as I have learned over the last thirty years, is money. If you have enough money, you can kill any political initiative that you don't like or buy enough votes to turn the legislation you like into law. It's sad, but that's how Washington politics work.

Many of the rich of Puerto Rico contributed to the statehood movement in order to promote their personal agenda with the PNP party (which favors statehood), while working behind the scenes against statehood to avoid paying federal income and estate taxes. When push came to shove, these power brokers always kept statehood just out of arm's reach for the rest of us. Case in point, I heard this story from a couple of sources but cannot verify it because it's cloaked in secrecy. Back in 1998, right after the Young Bill failed to get a vote in the Senate, one of our former governors was invited to speak to the leadership of both parties of Congress. Because our effort with the Young Bill had failed and I guess some members of Congress felt sorry for us, he was offered a kind of "consolation prize."

The proposal was simple. Congress offered to consider legislation that would reclassify Puerto Rico as an "incorporated territory." Puerto Rico would no longer be a "possession," waiting on the whims of the US Congress. It would still technically remain a colony, but incorporation would put Puerto Rico on a path toward self-determination and statehood.

After reviewing the offer with the key players of our group, the former governor came back to US Congress and told them no. Why did he refuse? Incorporated territories are subject to federal income and estate taxes. IRS Section 933 would no longer apply in Puerto Rico.

Many members of Congress were very much aware of this "I am for it until I become against it" attitude. That is why they continue to insist that Puerto Ricans can't decide on what they want. While they were happy to take our money to promote our statehood issue, many would ask me quietly with a smile, "Is it for real this time? Or is this going to be another beauty contest?" Meaning: "Do you really want statehood, or are you pushing this just so you can help elect your candidate in as governor?"

Besides our group's persistent indecision, another thing that didn't sit well with me was how our message was promoted. We often adopted a "poor me" approach when presenting our statehood case to the US Congress. The message largely stuck to these talking points:

- Puerto Ricans are currently second-class US citizens, and they deserve the full constitutional citizenship that other US citizens have.
- Puerto Rico lags behind all of the fifty states economically, with a per capita income less than half of that of Mississippi.
- Even though there are decisions made in the US Congress every day about Puerto Rico, the island has no voting representation in either chamber.
- Puerto Ricans are drafted in the armed forces of the US and die for America in foreign wars, but they cannot vote for their commander-in-chief.

The above are all good arguments in favor of statehood, but the problem is that they do not speak to the issues that really matter to members of Congress. As I have mentioned in previous chapters, if you want to sell something to somebody, you need to find the reason why your idea is good for the buyer, not just the seller. You have to tell Congress why Puerto Rican statehood is good for America, not just why it is good for Puerto Rico. Taking this "poor me" approach is like an insurance salesman telling his customer: "Please buy this policy because my rent is due this month and I need the commission."

For years, I have been trying to enhance our official message by including reasons why it is important for America for Puerto Rico to be a state, but it appears that no one wants to listen. Recently, I put together a very brief "business plan" as to how we should enhance our message and change how we structure our operation (see the political business plan in the appendix).

But it may be too late. We have been trying to achieve statehood for Puerto Rico now for about thirty years, and, in my opinion, we are now much closer to political sovereignty through independence than we have ever been. And the only people we need to thank for this condition is ourselves! Here is why: About ten years ago, Puerto Rico had close to four million residents. Today, we are lucky if we have three million. Most of those who left the island went to the mainland US because they were tired of being second-class citizens and moved to where they could be "full" American citizens and enjoy full federal benefits, which residents of Puerto Rico are still not entitled to.

Likewise, the Young Bill proved beyond a shadow of a doubt that there was no "commonwealth" or *estado libre asociado* (free associated state), as Governor Muñoz Marín had called it so many years ago. We were still a colony, but the worst type of colony. We were a "possession," as the US Supreme Court called us, and as such we had no right to self-determination. We were subject to the plenary powers of Congress, and Congress could do with Puerto Rico as it saw fit.

As a result, those "commonwealthers" who believed that they were living in some kind of "free associated state" had to regroup and decide to push "a contract of free association" with the US, which other US territories in the Pacific have today.

But as the prospects of such a deal faded, a disillusioned majority of the PDP party suddenly began to favor independence. This is reflected by the fact that during the 2020 primary vote for governor, the PDP nominated a die-hard *independentista* as their candidate with the mayor of San Juan, who has the same leanings, taking second place. Between the two of them, they got 77 percent of the PDP primary vote.

The 2020 vote is not an aberration: it's a trend. Over the last thirty years, the elections have swung back and forth between the PDP and the PNP, with each one getting close to 50 percent of the vote. The PIP, the independence party, typically received about 5 percent of the vote. In 2016, however, the statehood candidate for governor, Ricky Rosselló, got only 41 percent of the vote. That means that close to 60 percent of the Puerto Rico voters preferred a political status for Puerto Rico other than statehood.

And finally, in my opinion, from keeping my ear to the pulse and listening to people as to from where "the wind is blowing," the general desire of Puerto Ricans, who are still left on the island, has been moving in the direction of independence—especially since the president of the United States came to Puerto Rico after Hurricane Maria and threw paper towels at the residents.

But even if statehood is currently out of favor, the US should be wary of what could happen if the relationship between the island and the mainland doesn't change for the better in the near future. With so many Puerto Ricans wanting more say in their own affairs, the door is open for another economic superpower to step in and give the people what they want.

As it happens, one such nation—China—has been investing heavily in the Caribbean over the past decade and is starting to cast its eye toward Puerto Rico. If America doesn't wake up to this imminent threat, they may suddenly find their prized "possession" firmly and irretrievably in China's grasp.

SELF-DETERMINATION

AS I FINISH THIS BOOK AT THE END OF 2021, IT SEEMS CLEAR THAT THE people of Puerto Rico, who were once hoping for statehood, have concluded that "they" (the Americans) don't want "us" (Puerto Rican residents) … and that's okay.

I believe the people of Puerto Rico have had enough of the false promises made by those promoting statehood for the island—myself included. They are tired of all the bull being thrown at them, so they have decided instead to take the bull by the horns. They are rejecting the concerns of vested interests—the CFCs and other tax dodgers— that have kept Puerto Rico a colony for more than a century. Hurrah for the people of Puerto Rico! Perhaps we are about to see another *Grito de Lares* moment after a 150 year wait.

Interestingly, Puerto Rico's shift away from statehood is taking place just as Washington seems interested in the idea again. In the 2020 US presidential election, many Democrats advocated for a plan to annex Puerto Rico and Washington, DC as states. If they won the White House and Congress, they promised they would make it a priority. Of course, their motives were far from benevolent. Adding Puerto Rico and DC as states would allow them to shove four more Democratic senators down the throats of the Republican minority. That kind of partisan move sounds like something Mitch McConnell would do, but American politics has become something of a blood sport. That being said, in his first year in office, President Biden did reestablish a task force on Puerto Rico in order to address some the island's issues.

But in their political calculations, have Democrats considered the opinions of the Puerto Rican people? To make Puerto Rico a state, Democrats will need a Puerto Rican governor who wants statehood, a resident commissioner who wants statehood, and most of all a majority of the Puerto Rican people to vote in favor of state-hood. Unfortunately for Democrats, the trends are clearly moving in the opposite direction. In the last three elections over the course of the last twelve years, the three Puerto Rico governors from the PNP party, which is the statehood party, received the following percentages of the total vote:

- Luis Fortuño (2008): 53%
- Ricardo Rosselló (2016): 41%
- Pedro Pierluisi (2020): 33%

Directionally, the message is clear: In 2008, 53 percent of the people of Puerto Rico wanted a statehood governor. Twelve years later, in 2020, that percentage had dropped to 33 percent. For advo-cates of Puerto Rican statehood, sentiment is moving in the wrong direction. In the 2020 referendum, the split between the statehood "yes" or "no" vote was precisely 50.5 percent in favor of statehood and 49.5 percent against. Some may spin this as 52 percent in favor versus 48 percent against, which is fair if you do not count those who left that part of the ballot blank. Either way, you still have about half of the people of Puerto Rico who don't want statehood and only 32 percent who voted for a statehood governor. The numbers speak volumes, and they don't bode well for the pro-statehood camp.

At the same time, both the Puerto Rican House and Senate have gained a significant majority of members who openly promoted a political status *other* than US statehood in 2020. Most mayors elected in 2020 were also not in favor of statehood. In my fifty years as a businessman and resident of Puerto Rico, I have never seen such a dramatic rejection of both statehood and the major incumbent political parties. The people of Puerto Rico have spoken. In a true democracy, we would be on our way to independence, preferably through a "free association" agreement with the United States. Unfortunately, the political situation in Puerto Rico is far more complicated. You've had an insider's view of this complexity through the stories I've shared in this book. It's often difficult to know Puerto Rican voters' true allegiances. In yet another example of this, Puerto Rico's former governor, who supposedly favored statehood, supported an incumbent president of the United States, Donald Trump, who was decidedly against statehood for Puerto Rico.

Consequently, when I hear my friends in the US Congress tell me that the people of Puerto Rico can't decide what they want, I have no choice but to listen carefully. In previous chapters, I've called these statements unfair because the people of Puerto Rico have been given neither the opportunity nor the right to self-determination. The US Congress cannot be blamed for perceiving our statehood efforts up to this point as a farce. They have been. But are things finally changing in Puerto Rico? Because of the global economic pressures of the last few years, I believe they are. How these pressures influence the economic fortunes of Puerto Ricans over the next few years will determine what happens to the island's political status. Ever since I began my insurance and securities operations in Puerto Rico in 1970, I have heard the following statement related to economics on the island: When the mainland US sneezes, Puerto Rico catches pneumonia. In other words, when the US economy shrinks, the economy in Puerto Rico takes a nosedive. I've seen this happen time and again.

TIME FOR US LATINO VOTERS AND CONGRESS TO WAKE UP

Those who are not part of the US Latino community might assume that all Latinos in America are concerned about Puerto Rico's status. After all, the history of the status story is filled with discrimination and unfair treatment—topics of which US Hispanics are all too familiar. With this in mind, one might think Puerto Rico's status struggle could be a rallying point for US Latinos. Unfortunately, nothing could be further from the truth.

According to the Pew Research Center, the top issues for Hispanic voters in the 2020 US presidential election were the economy, health care, and the COVID-19 pandemic. Foreign policy was second to last on the list. And, of course, immigration is always at the forefront.

While stateside Puerto Ricans share many of these same concerns, there is one big difference: the political status of Puerto Rico is a top voting consideration for them. According to a 2020 national survey of mainland Puerto Ricans conducted by the Center for American Progress:

> The political status of Puerto Rico clearly influences the political decisions of those on the mainland. Nearly three-quarters of Puerto Ricans overall say they would be more likely rather than less likely to support a candidate for office who endorsed statehood for Puerto Rico. This includes 77 percent of both Republicans and Democrats, respectively, and 69 percent of political independents. Likewise, 70 percent of those who initially support options for Puerto Rico other than statehood still say they would be more likely to support a candidate for office who endorses making Puerto Rico a state.
>
> Interestingly, this overall figure rises to 86 percent of Puerto Ricans who are more likely to support a candidate who endorsed statehood using a fuller description noting "that the people of Puerto Rico would have the same rights as every other American and have five

members of Congress and two US senators representing them in Washington, DC."

The estimated 5.8 million Puerto Ricans living in the US, compared with only 3.2 million on the island. Puerto Ricans now make
up 1.78 percent of America's total population and 9.6 percent of
America's Latino population. They are the second-largest Latino
group in the US after Mexican Americans. But imagine if the voting
power of the entire Hispanic community in the United States, which
tops sixty-two million, were aligned around a change of status for
Puerto Rico. Now *that* could bring about real and lasting change!

If Puerto Rico were to become a US state, there would be two
more Latino senators and four more Latino representatives—and
most of them would be Democrats, which is how most Latinos politically identify today. Just think about how that change could help
promote top Latino issues. As of the writing of this book in 2021,
there are forty-seven members of the 116th United States Congress
who are Latino or Hispanic Americans—forty are in the House and
four are in the Senate. The final three members are territorial delegates. Some of them hold leadership positions in their chambers,
but the congressman from Puerto Rico territory, called the resident
commissioner, does not have a vote except in his or her committee—
and only if his or her vote is not a deciding one on an issue. In other
words, if you live in a territory of the United States, not only are you
a second-class US citizen, but you are also a second-class legislator
as far as Congress is concerned. Currently, geography decides the
value of American citizenship and the influence a legislator can have
among his or her fellow legislators. This is classic racial discrimination, as clearly illustrated in the "Insular Cases" that have driven US
Supreme Court decisions on this issue—but this is a different matter
for a different book.

As is the case in American politics, money matters when it comes
to legislation. US multinational corporations shower members of
Congress with campaign contributions in order to encourage opposition to any initiatives that promote sovereignty for Puerto Rico. The
island has more than three hundred Controlled Foreign Corporations
(CFCs), most of them "Big Pharma" and many which have few or no

employees in Puerto Rico but are still allowed to funnel tens of billions of dollars of profit from their worldwide subsidiaries through their Puerto Rican CFCs in order to avoid most of their US federal taxes obligations.

It's a sweet deal for these companies. But if Puerto Rico's status changes, this tax haven disappears for these shell corporations. That's why Washington, DC lobbyists for these corporations have issued specific marching orders to the Democratic Party leadership: If any member of Congress decides to run on a promise to make Puerto Rico a state, they will reduce or eliminate their multimillion-dollar political contributions immediately.

When it comes to Puerto Rico's sovereignty, money talks... loudly. As I covered in depth in my book *Pay to the Order of Puerto*, the tremendous influence of these multibillion CFCs prevents an honest debate about how to finally settle the political status of Puerto Rico—this while these companies pocket billions annually and cheat American taxpayers out of significant tax revenue.

Let me offer some personal stories to drive home the point:

During the 2020 election, I was talking to a friend who was running for the Senate in a state with a large Puerto Rican population. I said to him, "If you want to win the next election, go to every radio and TV station that caters to Puerto Ricans and tell them that if you are elected, you will make it your priority to make Puerto Rico a state."

His response was, "Alex, if I do that, the Senate leader will kill me because I am only allowed to say, 'I will support whatever the people of Puerto Rico decide.'"

We can all read between the lines here. The CFCs, using their enormous budgets, will confuse the issues so much that a status referendum in Puerto Rico will be inconclusive. They have done this time and time again. If you need further proof, just take a look at how the Young Bill was structured and the results of the last ten referendums.

I had a similar personal experience when I invited members of Congress to ski near my home in Vail, Colorado. My goal was to build support for Puerto Rico decolonization. At one of these events, the Speaker of the House participated. I remember his words almost verbatim: "Alex, you are talking up statehood too much here. Remember, we've got many millions in campaign contributions from the CFCs that operate in Puerto Rico, and if Puerto Rico becomes a state, we will lose those contributions, and we need them to win elections."

His message could not have been clearer.

This is not to say that all members of Congress are afraid to support decolonization of Puerto Rico. I know many who have defied warnings from lobbyists and their own parties and become champions for Puerto Rico's cause. Perhaps the time I spent with some of them on the ski slopes had something to do with their decision to break ranks and do the right thing. I'd like to think so, and I salute them. I just wish there were more brave individuals in Congress. In the meantime, the "oldest colony in the New World," as Puerto Rico is called, leaves America standing proudly as *the last country in the world* to still "own" a major colony—one which is has held for more than 120 years! This seems more than a bit hypocritical coming from a nation that prides itself on being called "the land of the free, and the home of the brave." And let's not forget who benefits from all this besides the CFCs: China, quietly watching, biding its time, and building like mad in the Caribbean, Central America, and South America as part of its ambitious Belt and Road Initiative. America's biggest adversary is waiting to strike at the right moment to take control of "America's Last Fortress."

In fifty years or so, when historians revisit this period of decline in American history, what will they say about those politicians who sold America's long-term, strategic security to the Chinese for a few paltry campaign contributions that allowed them to enjoy another two to six years in the US Senate or House? In that future, it will become crystal clear which politicians stood on the right and wrong side of history in the beginning of the twenty-first century—and it won't paint a pretty picture of those who put money before the country. Of course, this means Americans will still be writing their own history books fifty years in the future, which is looking increasingly questionable. Food for thought.

One of the issues that effects the severity of these economic cycles is that Puerto Rico has an elastic population. Translated, this means that when a Puerto Rican loses their job, as a US citizen, they can pick up and move to Orlando or New York or Chicago and look for a job there. And if they leave the island for the mainland, they are likely to find a job that pays a lot more money. A telltale statistic illustrating this trend is the unemployment rate in Puerto Rico, which has hovered between 15 percent and 20 percent for decades. It doesn't plummet with the booms, and it doesn't spike with the busts. When things are bad, unemployed Puerto Ricans flee the island. When things are good, they don't come back home. Over the last ten years, the population of Puerto Rico has shrunk by approximately 25 percent, and the exodus has continued in the wake of recent disasters. But this is only a part of Puerto Rico's woes. A November 2020 American University study called "The Impact of the COVID-19 Pandemic in Puerto Rico," stated that "the coronavirus is magnifying the territory's multilayered economic and social crisis."

> The island has been struggling for years to restructure $120 billion public debt, pension obligations, and losses as it also continues to recuperate from the destruction that was caused by Hurricanes Irma and Maria in 2017 and a series of earthquakes in January 2020. The pandemic also comes in the aftermath of a political crisis that resulted in the resignation of the Governor Ricardo Rosselló in August 2019.

> Puerto Rico has been hit hard by widespread unemployment resulting from the response to the pandemic. Even before the pandemic, 94,000 Puerto Ricans (36.2 percent of residents) were unemployed, and between March 16th and 30th, approximately 76,928 additional Puerto Ricans applied for unemployment benefits. Loss of employment is also associated with poor health. Therefore, the lack of employment during COVID-19 exacerbates existing disparities. Given these challenges, Gov. Wanda Vazquez took rapid action aimed to contain the coronavirus pandemic.

Note that the unemployment rate has now reached 36.2 percent even as some estimate that an additional three hundred thousand

Puerto Ricans will leave the island between 2020 and 2024 to seek better opportunities elsewhere. I'm not sure that the word "magnifying" quite does this change justice; it is an epic amplification of an already dire problem. All of this means that there will be less tax collection, less consumer activity, less demand for housing, less demand for services, less money for infrastructure and other public services, and more dependence on federal transfer payments. This, in turn, means there will be far fewer dollars circulating in the Puerto Rican economy. This will be exaggerated by the diminished multiplier effect on those dollars. For the statehood movement, these changes have big implications because many of the expats who now live on the mainland US favored statehood when they lived in Puerto Rico. As the increase in Puerto Rico's unemployment rate continues, more Puerto Ricans will be leaving the island, with more consumers taking their money with them. There will be less money left behind here to drive the economy.

All of these pressures feed the rising sense among Puerto Ricans that it is time to take control of their own destiny, be it through "free association" or independence. The Chinese were probably very happy with the results of the Puerto Rican elections in 2020; the outcome only moves the island closer to independence and further away from statehood. The deeper the divide grows between Puerto Rico and the United States, the more leverage China has. And if Puerto Rico's move away from statehood continues, the island's sovereignty through independence might become a reality—and sooner than any of us expect. This would give the Chinese an opportunity to onboard Puerto Rico to its Belt and Road Initiative with massive infrastructure investments, loans, etc.—all of which allow them to infiltrate America's last fortress in stealth mode. It would be an extraordinary geopolitical tragedy for the United States with devastating long-term economic, political, and security implications. Remember, China already has a substantive presence in South America, Central America, and the Caribbean. Puerto Rico would have an exponential impact on their growing control in the region.

China may not be as happy with the elections on the mainland US, though, because Biden and the Democratic Congress have put the plan to make Puerto Rico a state back on the table.

There is historical precedent for Congress acting to prevent foreign influence in Puerto Rico. Regarding the US citizenship question in 1917, Senator Jones was quoted as saying, "It is in America's national strategic interest to do so because it has cost a lot of American lives and treasure putting down rebellions in Cuba and the Philippines, and US citizenship will help America make Puerto Rico peaceful." Why would the US Congress not take the same approach to Puerto Rico's statehood in order to keep China from controlling the Caribbean? They should, and I still believe that with the right president in the White House, a Congress that looks at what is right for America, and with a Puerto Rico that might finally see that America does want them; there is still a chance that it could happen. Then, all US citizens and corporations in Puerto Rico would pay their fair share of taxes and not get rich on the tax boondoggles that are not good for either America's national security or Puerto Rico's economic development.

That said, if a majority of the Puerto Rican people decide on their own that they don't want statehood, I will respect their opinion and support whatever path they choose. For me, a clear path for Puerto Rico's self-determination is paramount. I'd rather see Puerto Rico make its own mistakes than have a political status shoved down their throats when half the population doesn't want it. That would be a travesty.

I don't know what Puerto Rico's relationship with the US will be in the future, but one thing is for sure: Puerto Rico's current colonial status is on its way out. Unless America's leadership wakes up—and soon—political independence for the island is imminent, in my opinion. America must decide whether it wants to retain its influence in Puerto Rico or cede its last fortress in the Caribbean to a rapidly ascendant Chinese.

In February of 2021, as part of the US Council on Foreign Relations Transition 2020 Series examining the major issues confronting the Biden-Harris administration, a panel discussed "Confronting the China Challenge." One member of the panel was Minxin Pei, a Chinese American political scientist and expert in governance in China, US-Asia relations, and democratization in developing nations. Here were his thoughts when he was asked about China's foreign policy goals:

> I see three things driving Chinese policy. One is perceived American decline. This has been a very important theme in driving Chinese foreign policy thinking. The second is perceived opportunities…and I single out two. The South China Sea Island building is one of the gray zone areas where they saw an opportunity where they could do what they wanted without encountering serious pushback. Obviously, they miscalculated. The other is Belt and Road, which is not exactly about infrastructure, it's really about neglect by the West of developing countries. And the third factor driving is really [Chinese President] Xi Jinping himself. This is a man who has a lot of appetite for risk, and he's single handedly really made a set of decisions I don't think his predecessor would have made.

What do you get when you couple Puerto Rico's waning interest in statehood, America's inability to act in either the island's best interest *or* its own self-interest in preserving a crucial strategic stronghold in the Caribbean, *and* a rising China with an audacious new leader? In my opinion, you get a perfect storm. And how do you prepare for a storm? You stock up, gather everyone together, and hunker down in a strong, safe place. You can ask the Puerto Ricans for further guidance. They're quite expert at surviving all kinds of storms. In fact, the official residence of the governor of Puerto Rico is *La Fortaleza* (The Fortress) in San Juan. It was built between 1533 and 1540, long before America became a country. It might be time for a visit.

"I WANT TO BE IN AMERICA. EVERYTHING FREE IN AMERICA!"

When I came to the United States as a nineteen-year-old, escaping the horrors of Communist Yugoslavia and earlier Nazi-occupied Belgrade, I was your typical, idealistic, wide-eyed immigrant—straight out of a movie. I had only $20 in my pocket but was giddy to finally be in the land of opportunity—a land that made millionaires out of those who dared to dream and work hard. I believed wholeheartedly in that promise and for me the American dream has come true.

If anyone had told me back then I would move to Puerto Rico, marry two Puerto Rican women, and have my kids on this beautiful island, I would have laughed in disbelief. However, if they added that my unique journey would lead me to passionate activism for Puerto Rico's self-determination, I would have told them they were just plain crazy. But life is full of interesting twists and turns, so here we are.

My own immigrant story has given me a unique perspective on Puerto Rico's rich and diverse culture. Their society is more multicultural European than other islands in the Caribbean. Their basic nature, in my opinion, is peaceful. Perhaps that's why they never really had an organized military rebellion against any of their colonizers.

Puerto Rican families hold values that generally tend to be conservative, so it is somewhat surprising that most Puerto Ricans have been typecast as Democrats—perhaps because of a wider bias about the Latino vote. Both Republicans and Democrats, who believe that the additional congressional seats Puerto Rico would add, would go to the Democrats would be wise to remember their history. Residents of Hawaii were once typecast as Republicans and are mostly Democrats today. Alaskans were once typecast as Democrats and are now mostly Republican. Things change, and neither political party should place too much weight on the idea that Puerto Rican statehood will mean a permanent change in the balance of US congressional power.

It seems to me that this type of stereotyping is still common in the United States—both inside and outside of politics. From where I sit, Americans seem to be stuck in a sort of 1957-Broadway-musical view of the island and its people. Yes, I'm talking about the iconic, multi-award winning and beloved *West Side Story*, which was recently brought back to life as a film released by none other than

Hollywood legend, Steven Spielberg. A rich and provocative discussion of *West Side Story*'s place in American culture appeared in the December 1, 2021, *New York Times*, just before the film's release. Called "The Great 'West Side Story' Debate," the article explores the long-held criticism that the original show stereotyped Puerto Ricans. Especially of interest to me was this response by Carina del Valle Schorske when a fellow panelist suggested that composer Leonard Bernstein loved and admired Latin music and tried to meld some of it into his score:

> I'm quite familiar with a broad range of Latin rhythms, and I don't hear or see the influence—unless you're counting the Spanish paso doble on the rooftop....It's good to know that someone was at least *trying* to do their homework after [lyricist Stephen] Sondheim confessed he'd "never even met a Puerto Rican."

Ouch! If you have the time, the entire discussion is worth a read. Truth is, there are so many iconic scenes and lines from *West Side Story*. Who can forget the choreography and music of "I want to be in America. Everything free in America." Just makes you want to sing and dance, right? Unfortunately, the phrase reinforced a powerful "freeloaders" stereotype that still haunts Puerto Rico today. Ask any Puerto Rican taxi driver what they think of *West Side Story*, and they'll give you an earful.

And besides, based on my experience watching Wall Street and US corporations use Puerto Rico as a tax shelter, I think *West Side Story* has it backward. It's not the Puerto Ricans who are freeloaders. If I die and come back to this world as a playwright or musical maestro, I might put together a little musical called *Wall Street Story* about how US businesses and lobbyists have repeatedly and deliberately destroyed the Puerto Rican sovereignty movement in order to stuff their pockets with billions of dollars that should have gone into the US Treasury. "I want to be in Puerto Rico. Everything tax free in Puerto Rico." Okay, the rhyme scheme is off, but I'm working on it.

Actually, instead of writing the musical score myself, maybe La India could drop a new version of her song "Ese Hombre" and switch out all the lines about how her ex-boyfriend did her wrong for lyrics about how the US does Puerto Rico wrong. I like that! Or maybe Daddy Yankee, the hit reggaeton singer and songwriter, could write a follow up to his song, "Gasolina." His new version could remind Americans about how Puerto Ricans jump-started American culture. And finally, there's Lin-Manuel Miranda's *In the Heights*, the 2021 film adaptation of his groundbreaking, Tony-winning, 2008 play, which came years before his Broadway masterpiece *Hamilton*. With *In the Heights*, at least, we find a multidimensional depiction of American-Latino culture, created by the child of Puerto Ricans. Puerto Ricans have a rich history of achievement in the United States. To name a few:

- Seven hundred thousand Puerto Ricans have served in the US armed forces.
- Joseph Michael "Joe" Acabá was the first astronaut from the island.
- Top talent like Rita Moreno, Jennifer Lopez, Ricky Martin, and Mark Anthony came from Puerto Rico.
- Antonia Novello, a Puerto Rican, served as Surgeon General of the United States, the first Hispanic woman to do so.
- Sonia Sotomayor is the first Puerto Rican to become a US Supreme Court Justice.

I don't know exactly what Puerto Rico's relationship with the US will look like in the future, but I do know one thing for sure: Puerto Rico's current colonial status is on the way out. If America doesn't take a fresh and more realistic look at its important island neighbor and fix what's broken, there's a very good chance that "Amereeka" will be singing a very different tune in a few decades, and its rhythm will most likely be more Asian than Latin.

Afterword

Free Association and *Con la Mancha de Plátano*

THERE HAS BEEN A LOT OF THEORIZING BY ACADEMIC AND POLITICAL communities in Puerto Rico, and to some degree on the mainland US, about what the mysterious "free association" political status might actually look like. Some call it independence with America watching over the island's shoulder. Others call it nothing more than an "enhanced commonwealth." Most just scratch their heads and walk away confused.

Having just read my book, you probably realize that I believe the people of Puerto Rico only have two choices in their quest to achieve sovereignty—that is if they really want to stop being an American "possession" (as defined by Supreme Court decisions). The people of Puerto Rico must choose between political independence and statehood. Of course, there is still no guarantee that the US Congress will honor the choice of the Puerto Rican people. Remember, American politicians have full plenary power over this key decision, which means Puerto Rico is not truly self-governing.

America's imperialist possession of Puerto Rico and the implications of the island's colony status were on display quite recently with the handling of the island's debt crisis. The Puerto Rico Oversight, Management, and Economic Stability Act (PROMESA) is a US federal law that was enacted in 2016 to establish a financial oversight board, a process for restructuring debt, and expedited procedures for approving critical infrastructure projects in order to manage the Puerto Rican debt crisis. Through PROMESA, the US Congress established and appointed a Fiscal Control Board (FCB), to oversee the island's debt restructuring. Puerto Ricans call the FCB *la junta*—a term that will be familiar to anyone who has watched a military group take control by force. To begin repaying the debt, the FCB approved a fiscal austerity plan for 2017-2026 that cuts deeply into Puerto Rico's public service budget, including cuts to health care, pensions, and education. By May 2017, with $123 billion in debt owed by the Puerto Rican government and its corporations, the FCB requested the immediate appointment of a federal judge to resolve the "largest bankruptcy case in the history of the American public bond market."

A hundred years ago, there were many imperialist countries that possessed colonies. I was talking with Representative Newt Gingrich about this topic back in the 1990s, just before he became Speaker of the House. We were in Atlanta, and I remember his words clearly: "Today, America is the only country in the world that still oversees a major colony: Puerto Rico. And that is an embarrassment. Even the Soviet Union gave up its colonies!"

But if Puerto Rico chooses pure independence, without any help from America, the island takes a big risk. It might do very well, but there is always a chance it could become the next Haiti. Here is where the mysterious "free association" concept comes into play. In Spanish, one would describe the "free association" relationship as *juntos pero no revueltos*—together but not so close. In other words, Puerto Rico would no longer be a US colony or possession. It would be an independent nation but still in business with America.

If a referendum on Puerto Rico's political status were to be held in the near future, which is my sincere hope, I would like to see two choices on the ballot:

1. Independence with "free association"
2. Statehood

Statehood is a straightforward choice that everyone can understand. Either Puerto Rico becomes the fifty-first star on a US flag or it doesn't. Simple. But "free association" starts with a wish list that must be cleared first by the US Department of Justice, second through a referendum in Puerto Rico, and third by the US Congress and White House. In Washington, we'd call that "a heavy lift." By definition, "free association" would be a contractual relationship (a treaty) between the sovereign nation of Puerto Rico and the United States of America. This formally concluded and ratified agreement between the two countries could be shaped by many ideas. Here is my wish list for the "free association" treaty between Puerto Rico and the US:

1. Puerto Rico must have sovereignty through political independence with contractual exemption from the Jones Act and the ability to freely engage in commercial treaties with the rest of the world without the approval of the US Congress or White House. The one exception, of course, would be treaties with China and its affiliates.

2. Puerto Rico must have continued US economic support at least equal to the current level with gradual decreases as the island's economy grows. There should be a thirty-year renewal clause based on economic progress.

3. Guaranteed and instant American citizenship should be granted to all newborns in Puerto Rico, provided that basic legal hurdles are overcome. If these hurdles cannot be overcome, then newborn Puerto Ricans will be given the status of nationals with unimpeded access to the US mainland.

4. If American citizenship is achieved, then Puerto Rico should have no vote in the United Nations because you can't have one group of US citizens voting against another.

5. Puerto Rico will maintain a non-voting representative in the US Congress.

6. Puerto Rico will have ongoing American military protection along with American management of the island's national post office system, customs, and others national systems.

7. Puerto Rico will have special tax benefits to attract US corporations, but the tax-haven status that many US CFCs enjoy today will have a "sunset clause." The government of Puerto Rico must be able to collect fair taxes from all of the participants in its economy so that it has sufficient tax money to build infrastructure and take care of its people.

How can these things be accomplished? Here is a basic outline of the steps as I see them:

1. Set up a 501(c)(4) nonprofit with the purpose of getting the above wish list approved by the Department of Justice, US Congress, and White House. This nonprofit would hire attorneys, consultants, lobbyists, and others to push these issues through the three branches of the US government.

2. Develop a system for funding the work on this process. This should allow for donations from both general supporters and US taxpayers.

3. Engage the Puerto Rican government as a partner in the process.

Next, the process would flow through these three stages:

1. Seek approval for the plebiscite from the US Department of Justice.

2. Hold a plebiscite, or non-binding referendum, in Puerto Rico with a ballot that offers two choices: statehood or independence through "free association."

3. Assuming a clear choice is made, supported by at least 60 percent of the Puerto Rican vote, lobby the US Congress to implement Puerto Rico's choice.

If this process is successful, Puerto Rico would be decolonized—no matter which choice wins in the referendum. That alone would be a major victory for the island.

There are many well qualified people who can flesh out the details of the basic outline I've created. It's simply meant to kick start the decolonization conversation and process. And the cost of all this? In my opinion, it is peanuts compared to what it accomplishes for the people of Puerto Rico. Here is my cost breakdown: I would guesstimate about three to five years of work at about $200,000 per month to pay lobbyists, experts, attorneys, administrators, and others. This should be paid by private sources through the nonprofit that I suggest forming at the beginning of the process. Any government support for this would be funded by taxpayers. I estimate the total private money expense to be about $12 million to $15 million plus campaign contributions. Does this mean the "free association movement" needs to recruit a bunch of rich people to support this project financially? Perhaps some, but today, campaign finance transcends the traditional "good ol' boy with deep pockets" benefactor, who is looking for some personal reward for making his or her contribution. With $50,000 today, you can get a grassroots contribution campaign started through social media that could bring in many millions of dollars to be deposited in the 501(c)(4) nonprofit, which would then drive the Puerto Rican sovereignty movement.

There are ten million Puerto Ricans between Puerto Rico and the US mainland. If only 240 thousand of them (that's only 2.4 percent) contributed $10 per year to this project, it would be fully funded. But how do you get the first $50,000 without bringing in the fat cats who would want to control the process? Well, if I were an Uber driver and deep in my heart really wanted sovereignty for Puerto Rico, I would look for a buddy that worked for a social media marketing company who had the same beliefs. Then, between the two of us, we would find an accountant, an attorney, and a sales and marketing person who might also feel the same way. So, we now have five true believers, but no money. If each of the believers went out and found four more believers, regardless of their occupations, we would have twenty-five believers. Since all the believers have good jobs, each could go to an ATM machine and withdraw $2,000 and send it to the 501(c)(4). Bingo! There is your seed money to start the cash rolling in.

I have talked a lot in *America's Last Fortress* about how any change in status must start with *el Pueblo de Puerto Rico*, the people of Puerto Rico. It is imperative that all decisions about the future of Puerto Rico rest in their hands, not those of fat-cat corporations and big-shot politicians in America. This is nonnegotiable. There is a saying in Puerto Rico, where plantains are an important crop and food source. It is *con la mancha de plátano*, which refers to the stubborn stain the plantain sap leaves on farmers' hands when the crop is being harvested. For *el Pueblo de Puerto Rico* the phrase *con la mancha de plátano* is a national cry that says we are Puerto Rican, and we have pride in our beautiful and unique culture and land. You see, the plantain stain is impossible to remove, just like the love Puerto Ricans have for their country.

Acknowledgments

I REALLY WANT TO THANK KATHY MEIS AND THE ENTIRE TEAM AT Bublish, Inc. They offer superb editing that can make a manuscript sing like Pavarotti. If you ever plan to publish a book, call Kathy and her team. They will help you publish professionally, and when you hold the final book in your hand, you will say, "Wow!"—just like I did!

Me, President Joe Biden, Luis Costas,
Ken McClintock, and Carlos Chardon

Senator Hillary Clinton and Me

Me next to Vice President Al Gore and others at lunch

Me and General Wesley Clark

Representative Steny Hoyer,
Odette, and Me

Odette, Representative Loretta Sanchez, and Me

Me, Odette, Howard Hills, Representative Bob
Lagomarsino and his wife Norma

Me and Senator Jim Inhofe

Me and Senator Trent Lott

President Clinton, Me, and others

Me, US Attorney General Richard Thornberg,
and Major General Felix Santoni

Me at a book signing

"Ski Instructor" Me and Representative Carolyn Maloney and her family

Me and Harvey Keitel

Senator Jay D. Rockefeller and Me

Attorney General Janet Reno, Me, and guest

Odette, Me, Representative Bob Lagomarsino and his wife
Norma. Wife of former head of OPIC, Mrs. Lura Hills and Melba
Fugueroa Esq. at her home in Old San Juan, Puerto Rico

Me, Mrs. Vicky Kennedy, and Senator Ted Kennedy

Senator Tom Daschle and Me

Representative Dick Gephardt and Me

Representative Paul Cook and his wife with Odette and Me

APPENDIX I

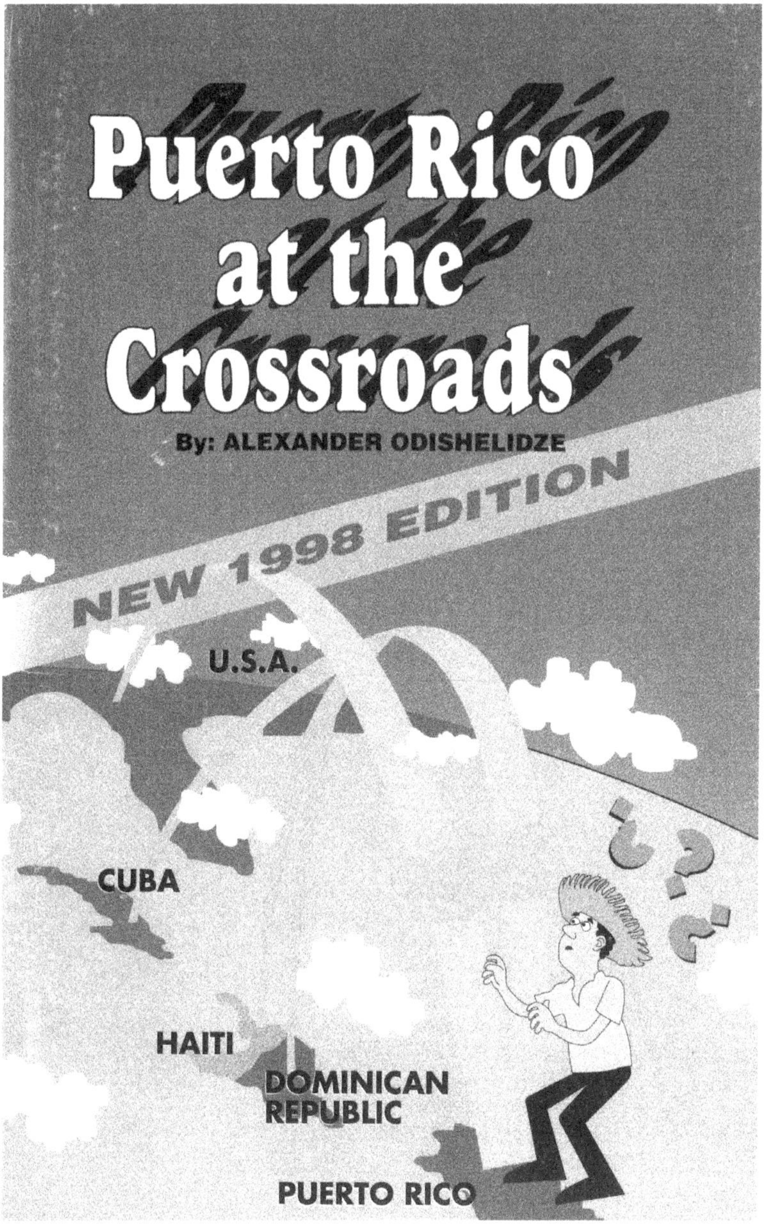
Puerto Rico
at the
Crossroads
By: ALEXANDER ODISHELIDZE
NEW 1998 EDITION
U.S.A.
CUBA
HAITI
DOMINICAN
REPUBLIC
PUERTO RICO

Price - $2.95

ISBN 0-9633405-5-7

$2.95

2ND EDITION - FEB. 1998

Publisher

EMPLOYEE BENEFITS ASSOCIATES, INC.
Publishing Division

El Caribe Bldg., Suite 1503 - #53 Palmeras St.
San Juan, Puerto Rico 00901
Phones: (787) 723-5535 / (787) 723-5349
Fax (787) 723-4772

For information or subscriptions
MONEY MASTERY NEWSLETTER
1-800-237-8400 Ext. 2001
For additional copies of this booket
1-800-237-8400 Ext. 2003

Contents

THE FINAL CHAPTER

SUMMARY OF THE KEY POINTS RELATING TO PUERTO RICO'S STATUS AND ITS IMPACT ON THE LOCAL ECONOMY

SUMMARY OF ECONOMIC POINTS RELATED TO STATUS

The Commonwealth Status Is a Very Costly Proposition for US Taxpayers

1. Prior to 1950, Puerto Rico had all the advantages it has today:
    a. Section 936 (it was section 931 prior to 1976)
    b. US citizenship
    c. Free access to US markets
    d. Political stability by being under the US flag.

Yet, prior to 1950, Puerto Rico had the lowest per capita income of any island in the Caribbean, lower than Haiti, Dominican Republic, Jamaica and much lower than Cuba. In those days, Puerto Rico was known as the "Poorhouse of the Caribbean."

2. What changed after 1950 was that the US decided to make Puerto Rico "The Shining Star in the Caribbean" in order to keep communism out of the region. The US accomplished this by allowing Puerto Rico to participate in the federal social benefits created by the Roosevelt New Deal.

In addition, in 1960, the US implemented the embargo against Castro's communist Cuba, which diverted US investment from Cuba to Puerto Rico and brought about two hundred thousand Cuban refugees who brought with them millions of dollars in capital which they invested in the local economy. They were businessmen and professionals, and they did for Puerto Rico's economy the same thing they did to South Florida's economy. By the early 1970s, Puerto Rico had the highest per capita income in the Caribbean.

3. In the early 1950s and 1960s, the following conditions were present:
   a. US Treasury was running a budget surplus.
   b. The world was in the Cold War.
   c. Castro was threatening the region with communism.
   d. Federal social benefits were being expanded.
   e. Access to US markets was limited due to tariffs and import restrictions.

4. Today, the situation is different:
   a. The US Treasury is running a budget deficit.
   b. The Cold War is over, but China's Belt and Road Initiative poses a new threat to the Caribbean and US.
   c. Federal Social benefits are more limited.
   d. Trade agreements no longer make free access to US markets such an economic advantage.
   e. Cuba is now opening up to Cuban American investors.

5. Though Puerto Rico contributes to the US federal Treasury, benefits have been reduced and might have contributed to the huge percentage of Puerto Ricans who have moved to the mainland US, where benefits are much more generous. Still, Puerto Rico has received billions in federal social benefits and transfers, and these benefits remain the main drivers of Puerto Rico's economy. Additional economic drivers include federal grants for roads and bridges, Federal Emergency Management Agency (FEMA) disaster relief money, and other infrastructure and social and fiscal benefits.

6. As Cuba has slowly opened up, it has begun to take a piece of Puerto Rico's international tourism industry and investment money has been redirected to other Caribbean islands.

7. Puerto Rico's debt crisis accompanied by multiple natural disasters have once again turned Puerto Rico into the "Poorhouse of the Caribbean."

8. In order for Puerto Rico to survive economically, it needs to get out of its current territorial/colonial status, and either move toward sovereignty as an independent nation or statehood. With sovereignty, Puerto Rico would be able to make its own treaties with foreign nations and develop its own economic drivers. It would not be subject to US laws that could have a negative effect on its economy. Under statehood, Puerto Rico would have assured political stability, voting representation in Congress, and a vote for the US president. This could attract new investment to the island and enable it to protect itself from adverse legislation through its representation in Congress. Statehood would also allow Puerto Rico to qualify for full federal social benefits like other states.

9. Right now, Puerto Rico is costing US taxpayers many billions of dollars per year with the sum continuously growing.

As an independent republic or a freely associated state, Puerto Rico would qualify for foreign aid. This would significantly reduce the cost of maintaining Puerto Rico, which is very expensive for American taxpayers.

As a state, Puerto Rico would pay more into the federal Treasury and gain the right to federal social benefits like all other US states. This would offset the current imbalance of unequal social benefits for Puerto Ricans and the high tax burden for mainland US taxpayers supporting those benefits.

Economic studies have shown that the first year of statehood would result in a net profit to US taxpayers of $2.72 billion and would exceed $100 billion over ten years.

Either of the above options would place Puerto Rico on a solid economic footing and save mainland US taxpayers billions of dollars.

PUERTO RICO
AT A GLANCE

PUERTO RICO AT A GLANCE

The Island
The size of Connecticut, 1,050 miles southeast of Miami.

Government
US territory with local self-government.

Citizenship
Puerto Ricans are US nationals with statutory American citizenship.

Language
English and Spanish are the island's official languages.

Society
Significant social and political integration with the US since 1898.

Education
One of the world's highest secondary enrollments.

Politics
High voter turnout for all elections.

Economy
Per capita income of $21,700 as of 2020.

Trade
Puerto Rico imported $21.2 billion and exported $16.8 billion in 2020. Total exports/imports have remained around $38 billion since 1994.

Transport

San Juan was once one of the world's ten busiest container ports. Today, it no longer ranks in the top fifty.

Defense

To date, more than two hundred thousand Puerto Ricans have served in the US military.

EDITOR'S NOTE

The bulk of the following article was originally written as a special March 1995 edition of my *Money Mastery* newsletter for our Puerto Rico subscribers at the time. It remains mostly intact but has been updated with pertinent new information and data. —*Alex Odishelidze (January 2021)*

The events that I describe in the next few pages could have profound impact on many US corporations, which in turn could impact their stock prices and the values of mutual funds that invest in them.

In addition, Puerto Rico is going through a transition period right now that could lead it toward statehood or independence. If over the next couple of years, Puerto Rico does move toward becoming a state or independent nation, there will be enormous investment opportunities there. Those who had inside information about Hawaii's impending statehood and invested there became multimillionaires by getting the jump on everybody else. The same scenario could come to pass with a change in Puerto Rico's status. For example, if Puerto Rico becomes a state, US and international investments there would be covered by the same political and economic guarantees provided to investors in other US states. If Puerto Rico becomes an independent nation, international investors would be able to freely invest there while US investors could take advantage of "OPIC insurance." This is insurance offered by the Overseas Private Investment Corporation (OPIC) established in 1971 and now called the US International Development Finance Corporation.

With this in mind, I decided to write this article to provide a thorough understanding of how this process is shaking out and discuss the potential traps that still lie ahead.

PUERTO RICO AT THE CROSSROADS

Reprinted from a March 1995 issue of *Money Mastery* with some minor modifications and updates.

PUERTO RICO AT THE CROSSROADS

Puerto Rico is currently sitting on an economic powder keg, with the fuse lit and getting dangerously close to the ignition point.

For example, as a result of the decrease in population over the past ten years and other economic challenges, many of Puerto Rico's real estate investments have lost substantial value. Additionally, as I predicted many years ago, GNMAs (mortgaged-backed securities guaranteed by the Government National Mortgage Association) and other bonds have collapsed leading to Puerto Rico's default on such instruments.

While the people of Puerto Rico and the US Congress continue arguing politics, telltale economic signals abound and indicate that things today are quite different from the way they have been over the last fifty years.

I do have an economic stake in Puerto Rico. And whether I like it or not, the events that will shape Puerto Rico's future are very much political in nature. So, in order for me to effectively discuss the island's economics, I must first discuss politics—both in Puerto Rico and stateside.

A New Breed of Congress

Today's US Congress is a different group than the ones that made the deal with Luis Muñoz Marín for Puerto Rico's commonwealth status way back in the 1940s, 50s, and 60s. In 2021, Congress (both Republican and Democrat) are dealing with a global pandemic, environmental threats, and political polarization. Most politicians couldn't care less about expressed or implied commitments to "clean up the current messy status of the 'territories' (Puerto Rico included)."

As long as Puerto Rico is a commonwealth, rather than a state or independent country, funding of its social benefits conspires with its commonwealth income tax system to create a perceived roadblock to balancing the US federal budget. These expenses are a luxury that the mainland taxpayers and members of Congress on both sides of the aisle are in no mood to continue.

Members of Congress are always thinking, "How can we cut expenses so I can bring more cash back home to my constituents?" The notion that Puerto Rico is too important to be guided by that question will lead to a rude awakening when it might be too late. In order for Puerto Rico to survive in the twenty-first century, our wakeup call has to be: "What worked yesterday, will no longer work tomorrow. If we keep hanging on to yesterday, we will all be in the poorhouse tomorrow!"

Only Reason to Stay a Colony

Section 936 has been phased out, but the same corporations that benefited from its tax shelter now have converted to controlled foreign corporations (CFCs), which enjoy most of the same benefits. Many other companies have opened shell corporations in Puerto Rico through which they can funnel their worldwide profits and avoid paying the US government taxes. As a result, more companies are paying less in taxes to the US today.

Though section 936 helped Puerto Rico develop its manufacturing base, which became the nucleus of its economy, it probably did more harm than good over the long run. After section 936 was phased out, it was replaced by another crutch, the CFCs. This magnified Puerto Rico's problems because under section 936 only profits realized in Puerto Rico were eligible for a tax credit. With CFCs, *all* global profits can be funneled through a Puerto Rico shell company and become eligible for the tax cut. This has kept the Puerto Rican economy dependent on tax gimmicks and prevented development of a solid, diverse economic base.

It has also justified the commonwealth, allowing Puerto Rico the luxury of playing out our politics based on a choice of status instead of addressing the real issues that impact our quality of life. With the crutches of section 936 and many US federal programs phased out, commonwealth status had gone from "the best of both worlds" to the "worst of all worlds."

Puerto Rico Is Just a Messy Issue to Clean Up

Many Puerto Ricans delude themselves into thinking that the US Congress is committed to "cleaning up the messy territories question." That is simply no longer true. If we don't decide whether we want independence or statehood, they will force the issue. Some of our more vocal "political experts," who still think that the US owes Puerto Rico something and that we are in a position to negotiate, are not in touch with today's realities.

It's Easy to Cut Off Your Nose to Spite Your Face

Before Puerto Rico became a commonwealth and Luis Muñoz Marín made his brilliant deal for Puerto Rico's economic development, Puerto Rico was the poorest nation in the Caribbean. Then, it became the richest. Today, we've lost that standing.

Muñoz Marín's genius was reflected in the fact that he could throw politics aside, and having spent all his life as an avid *independentista*, recognize that he had a moment of opportunity to transform Puerto Rico's economy by developing the commonwealth model through a closer alliance with the US. Had he not done what he did and continued to stubbornly hang on to and prevailed with his original ideals, Puerto Rico would probably be another Dominican Republic, or, worse yet, Cuba.

But do Puerto Rico's current politicians have the same foresight and courage of Muñoz Marín to recognize the crossroads we are at right now? Do they fully grasp the opportunity to lead Puerto Rico into the twenty-first century? Or will they continue their bickering and hang on to their outdated and unrealistic sacred cows—dragging us down with them?

What Is the Risk?

Anyone who has any economic commitment to Puerto Rico—anyone who owns a home, other real estate, or a business here—has got his or her hard-earned dollars on the line. Those dollars are currently hanging by a thread held by our politicians and their decisions as to where they want to lead Puerto Rico.

In the fifty-plus years that I have lived here, never has there been a time when our financial wellbeing has been so closely tied to Puerto Rico politics, our relationship with the US, and our status.

Section 936 Had Little Positive Impact on Our Economy

Earlier, I mentioned that section 936 did more harm than good for Puerto Rico's economy. To illustrate my point, in 1987, we had ninety-eight thousand employees working in manufacturing of which approximately twenty-five thousand employees worked for 936 companies while our total employment was 862,000. That means section 936 jobs accounted for 2.9 percent of all employment.

What this means to me is that our economy is no longer strictly driven by section 936 companies or CFCs. Other areas of Puerto Rico's economy—tourism, construction, retailing, services, finance, and others—have grown independent of those tax exemptions.

The problem is that most investors believe Puerto Rico's entire economy is propped up strictly by corporate tax exemptions. As a result, they are reluctant to invest in Puerto Rico. The perpetuation of the section 936 myth continues to prevent Puerto Rico from enjoying serious investment from both internal and external sources.

Here Is the Proof

Before section 936 was finally phased out, a 1994 economic study was conducted by Mr. Angel Ruiz PhD, dean of the School of Economics at InterAmerican University, and Mr. Edwin Meléndez PhD, who heads up an independent economic think tank in Cambridge Massachusetts. Though almost thirty years old now, much of what the study revealed holds true today.

- One of the points the study made was that the employment multiplier effect of section 936 company employment was less than 1.5, which is much lower than the 3 and 4 that had been estimated. The researchers also questioned the Congressional Budget Office's (CBO) estimate that elimination of section 936 would result in "a loss of 37% to 47% of the capital and production of 936 corporations by the year 2000." Instead, they predicted that the reduction in investment and production caused by a phaseout of section 936, would help Puerto Rico's economy grow by only 2% less over the coming seven years. This would result in average growth of 0.44% instead of a projected growth of 2.62%.
- The study also concluded that the total employment reduction as a result of a decline in growth would be only 92,000 workers less than if section 936 remained alive and well. Dr. Ruiz and Dr. Meléndez observed that the CBO study did not consider efforts to offset section 936 losses through aggressive development of other industries.
- The key point that Dr. Meléndez and Dr. Ruiz made in their study was that if we took into consideration the growth of

other non-936 industries (after elimination of section 936), then the reduction in capital by section 936 companies would only amount to 16%. As a result, of this other economic activity, Puerto Rico's unemployment rate would actually decrease from 15.88% in 1993 to 9.88% in the year 2000, actually increasing total employment by 227,000 workers by the year 2000. While the island's GNP would grow at a 1.92% rate. So, in fact, this study showed that the elimination of section 936 would actually be good for Puerto Rico's economy.

Another study, this one in 1993 by Professor Jaime Bofill, explored "The Impact of Federal Disbursements and Taxes in the Puerto Rican Economy" and showed that if Puerto Rico became a state, federal benefits would increase by $1.34 billion, which would positively impact Puerto Rico's GNP growth by 1.89 percent.

This was a fascinating point. If the elimination of section 936, based on the worst-case scenario (represented by the CBO study), would negatively affect Puerto Rico's GNP by 2 percent, and the $1.34 billion increase in federal benefits would boost GNP by almost 2 percent, then it stands to reason that full participation in US federal benefits (and federal tax program) as a state would be a better option than trying to hang on to tax shelters at all cost.

Federal Taxes Are Good for Economy

Therefore, if Puerto Rico becomes a state and federal taxes are implemented, we would only lose our proportionate share, which, on the basis of parity, might be very little indeed. If, on the other hand, Puerto Rico remains a commonwealth and US federal programs are cut, we could wind up with less than half of what we are getting now.

New Investment and Expanded Tax Base

The phaseout of tax shelters will spur new investment in Puerto Rico, which will create new jobs. But it will also dramatically expand our tax base, bringing in more revenue.

Once Fomento, Puerto Rico's Business Development Agency, is no longer focusing on promoting manufacturing, which benefits from tax shelters, it can easily promote business in many other areas such as financial services, information, communication, tourism, services (especially those exported to Latin America).

If the tax gimmicks were eliminated, Puerto Rico would also then have to compete based on its ability to create a good business climate—just like other US states and countries. This would mean revamping the island's labor laws to make them more "business friendly." Red tape would need to be reduced for business formation and new businesses. Infrastructure would need to be rebuilt—roads, power, water, schools, etc., so that Puerto Rico can be known as a good place to be in business.

Statehood Would Make Property Values Double

If it appeared that Puerto Rico were pursuing statehood, areas of real estate development and tourism would boom, and new investment would flow into Puerto Rico. The island would be able to attract more investment that might have gone to other Caribbean islands, because the permanent American flag would create confidence and security. But if we keep dillydallying with commonwealth status, Puerto Rico will be left in the dust. This is already happening.

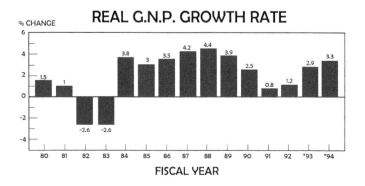

REAL G.N.P. GROWTH RATE

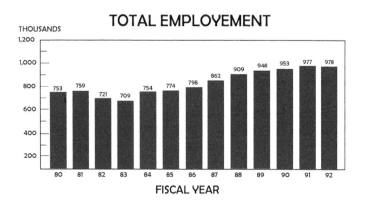

TOTAL EMPLOYMENT

Status = *State of Economy*

Puerto Rico's economy is greatly impacted by its status. I have prepared two graphs that illustrate the direction that I feel Puerto Rico's economy would take based on our politics moving us toward one side or the other. (See Graphs A and B). Keep in mind, since hard data was not used to construct these graphs (because even though we are certain that we will have changes in key economic factors that affect us, we still don't have the exact numbers representing those factors nor the exact effect they will have), we can only try to predict the direction but not the degree of change.

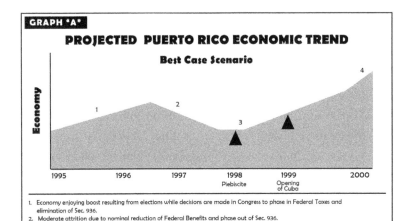

GRAPH "A"

PROJECTED PUERTO RICO ECONOMIC TREND

Best Case Scenario

1. Economy enjoying boost resulting from elections while decisions are made in Congress to phase in Federal Taxes and elimination of Sec. 936.
2. Moderate attrition due to nominal reduction of Federal Benefits and phase out of Sec. 936.
3. Plebiscite, with a solid majority in favor of Statehood.
4. Economic boost resulting from upcoming Statehood overcoming negative effect of Cuba Opening.

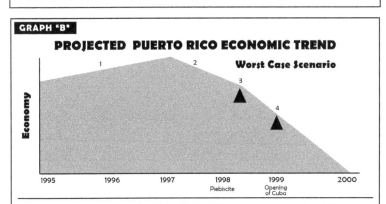

GRAPH "B"

PROJECTED PUERTO RICO ECONOMIC TREND

Worst Case Scenario

1. Economy enjoying boost resulting from elections related activity while decisions are made in Congress to reduce social benefits substantially to Puerto Rico and phase out Sec. 936.
2. Severe attrition because of phase out of Sec. 936 and rejection of Federal taxation in Puerto Rico resulting in severe Federal cuts and population loss.
3. Continuing attrition due to a lack of a clear majority for Statehood.
4. Additional economic shock to Puerto Rico due to Opening of Cuba resulting in diversion of Investment from Puerto Rico to Cuba.

Statehood Would Lead to an Economic Boom

If Puerto Rico were to become a US state, we would begin to see a boom in construction like we have never seen before. Hotels and beachfront condominium developments would spring up all over the island and begin selling at premium prices. This would spur activity in upscale shopping centers. Construction around those developments and many other industries would bloom and prosper. Rep. Neil Abercrombie from Hawaii once said to me, and I quote, "If Puerto Rico becomes a state, your biggest problem will be managing your economic growth."

On the other hand, if there is no clear majority for statehood in the next plebiscite and Puerto Rico holds on to its commonwealth status, we will continue economic decline. Under this worst-case scenario, we would lose most of our federal benefits and our economic future would be headed away from the benefits of being under the US flag, so we would no longer enjoy the "confidence" investor. Tourism and consequently construction would also continue to decline, bringing our retail industry down along with real estate prices.

Manufacturing would continue to erode because it would be dominated by our competition in the Caribbean, who can offer lower hourly wages. We also wouldn't have the tax base to rebuild our infrastructure to make us an attractive place to do business. With no clear path to statehood, our already fragile economy could shrink by twenty percent to thirty percent over the next five to ten years, making us once again the "Poorhouse of the Caribbean." (See Graph B).

Next Few Years Are Critical

The events over the next few years will either make or break personal financial fortunes of those who have an economic commitment to Puerto Rico.

Should we put our hard-earned dollars on the line for a status quo that is left over from another era? Or should we start planning now to protect our capital? The good news is, we still have time to plan.

The foregoing discussion has been an expression of my opinion, based on the information that I have gathered and processed personally over many years. I have no intention of defending my opinion as a statement of fact. My only intention is to share my opinion with my readers, and "if the shoe fits"…you can wear it or discard it as you will.

ADDENDUM

A TIME FOR DECISIONS

Since March of 1995, when *Puerto Rico at the Crossroads* was first published in my *Money Mastery* newsletter, there have been many developments along with ongoing predictions, some of which have come to pass.

For the above reason, residents of Puerto Rico need to be more cognizant of what those events really represent to their economy and personal financial wellbeing.

In order to effectively protect and enhance our assets in Puerto Rico, we need to be aware of the meaning of those events, and how those events drive new trends, which in turn impact our businesses and investments.

Let me briefly go over some of these events and discuss their impact.

I. Elimination of Section 936

In the March 1995 edition of *Money Mastery*, I predicted the death of section 936. Its demise was tacked on to President Clinton's minimum wage bill, which included an incentive to help small businesses cope with the increase in the minimum wage. This incentive was paid for with the former tax credits of 936 companies. The bill eliminated the passive income tax exemption for 936 companies. It phased out the income-based tax credit over two years and the wage-based tax credit over eight years.

In the long term, the elimination of this tax gimmick was good for Puerto Rico's economy because it helped lift the perception of a false economy and help build investment on a more solid economic base.

Government agencies like Fomento and the Government Development Bank had grown lazy, strictly relying on temporary tax gimmicks to promote a single industry, manufacturing, at the expense of other industries. Elimination of section 936 forced those agencies to seek viable alternatives, which in turn will helped develop other industries like services, banking, insurance, communications, and information.

Puerto Rico has a pool of well-educated and well-trained bilingual managers, professionals, skilled assembly workers, and technicians who can be developed for more industries than just manufacturing. As a matter of fact, Puerto Rico has a higher per capita percentages of college graduates than the mainland US.

As the two graphs on the following page indicate, those pharmaceutical companies that once threatened to leave Puerto Rico if section 936 were eliminated, have actually *increased* their employment in Puerto Rico from 25,127 employees in 1993 to 25,842 employees in 1994.

But that's not all. Dr. Ruiz and Dr. Meléndez updated their study to show that the elimination of section 936 would bring the unemployment rate down below 9 percent by 2000. If this happens, Puerto Rico will never have had such a low unemployment rate in its history.

EMPLOYMENT IN 936 CORPS

NUMBER OF EMPOYEES	1991	1992	1993	1994
		BEFORE OBRA 93		AFTER OBRA 93
Abbot	2,200	2,200	2,200	2,500
American Cynamid	1,121	1,201	1,295	1,169
American Home Products	1,000	1,000	903	1,000
Baxter	5,600	5,547	6,000	5,600
Bristol Myers Squibb	2,153	2,160	2,160	1,800
Eli Lilly	1,003	1,003	1,000	800
Johnson & Johnson	3,000	3,700	3,674	3,701
Merk	800	863	930	965
Pfizer	600	739	824	980
Rhone Poulenc Rorer	276	283	275	254
Schering Plough	1,400	1,293	1,294	1,300
SmithKline Beechman	991	828	828	728
Upjohn	672	686	666	661
Warner Lambert	1,580	1,632	1,800	1,900
TOTAL	24,387	25,127	25,842	25,352

SOURCE: CARIBBEAN BUSINESS

SAVINGS IN TAXES OF 936 CORPS

NUMBER OF EMPOYEES	1991	1992	1993	1994
(MILLIONS)		BEFORE OBRA 93		AFTER OBRA 93
Johnson & Johnson	$158	$212	$226	$247
Bristol Myers Squibb	$260	$173	$260	$187
Pfizer	$114	$126	$165	$184
Merk	$162	$182	$158	$168
Baxter	$94	$123	$128	$129
American Home Products	$122	$105	$122	$112
Abbott	$130	$106	$130	$111
Upjohn	$89	$77	$108	$84
Schering Plough	$65	$65	$66	$79
Warner Lambert	$15	$58	$17	$50
Eli Lilly	$88	$84	$64	$36
Rhone Poulenc Rorer	$10	$29	$21	$24
TOTAL	$3,297	$3,331	$3,459	$3,404

SOURCE: CORPORATION ANNUAL REPORTS

A simple example of why the current commonwealth status is bad for Puerto Rico's economy is reflected in minimum wage bill debates, which happen often on Capitol Hill.

Higher minimum wages can have a downside effect on employment, especially as it relates to small businesses. Since Puerto Rico is not a state, it does not qualify for the special incentives that stateside small businesses receive to help them offset the cost of minimum wage hikes. Yet, as a territory of the US, Puerto Rico has no choice but to comply with an increase in the minimum wage if it is mandated by Congress.

If Puerto Rico were a true freely associated state or an independent republic, our sovereignty would allow us to ignore US federally mandated minimum wage hikes and make legislative decisions based on our own national economic needs. But as a colony, we are forced to comply with US laws that could negatively impact our economy without receiving benefits to offset those negative impacts.

As a state of the union, we would enjoy all the offsetting benefits that such legislation might create for Puerto Rico. We would also be in a position to influence legislation with a projected six congressmen in the House of Representatives and two senators in the Senate.

II. Public Hearings in Washington and Puerto Rico Relating to Status and the Letter Signed by the Four Chairs of the Committees That Have Jurisdiction Over Puerto Rico

Public hearings in Washington and Puerto Rico in the mid-1990s demonstrated clearly that no matter how hard we have tried to circumvent reality; it has come back to slap us in the face.

Some politicians in Puerto Rico have refused to see the handwriting on the wall and continued to sing the same old tune. Back in the mid-1990s they did this by sacrificing the wellbeing of the Puerto Rican people in order to stay in power.

To demonstrate how out of step some of these politicians have been, here are some quotes from those public hearings in Puerto Rico and from the text of the letter signed by the four chairs of the committees with jurisdiction over Puerto Rico back in the mid-1990s:

1. *"…Certain elements of the commonwealth option, including permanent union with the United States and guaranteed US citizenship, can only be achieved through full integration into the US leading to statehood. Other elements of the commonwealth option on the ballot, including a government-to-government bilateral pact which cannot be altered, either are not possible or could only be partially accomplished through treaty arrangements based on separate sovereignty"* (see the letter signed by the four chairs of the committees in the "Supplement" section).

2. *"It is incontrovertible that Puerto Rico's present status is that of an unincorporated territory subject in all respects to the authority of the United States Congress under the Territorial Clause of the US Constitution"* (see letter signed by the four chairs).

3. *"The results of the November 14, 1993, vote (plebiscite) indicates that it is the preference of those who cast the ballots to change the present impermanent status in favor of a permanent political status based on the full self-government"* (see letter signed by the four chairs).

4. *"Is important to recognize that the existing commonwealth of Puerto Rico structure for local self-government, and any other measures which Congress may approve while Puerto Rico remains an unincorporated territory,*

are not unalterable in a sense that is constitutionally binding upon a future congress" (see letter signed by the four chairs).

5. *"Ultimately, Congress alone can determine federal policy with respect to self-government and self-determination for the residents of Puerto Rico"* (see letter signed by the four chairs).

6. *"The results of the locally administered 1993 vote (plebiscite) are useful in this regard, but in our view are not definitive beyond what has been stated above. The question of Puerto Rico's political status remains open and unresolved"* (see letter signed by the four chairs).

7. *"Congress can now impose English as the only language in Puerto Rico while Puerto Rico continues as a territory"* (Rep. Patrick Kennedy; public hearings held on March 23, 1996, in San Juan, PR).

8. *"Puerto Rico is a US territory and only US Congress can make decisions relating to Puerto Rico"* (Rep. Don Young; public hearings held on March 23, 1996, in San Juan, PR).

9. *"I don't know of any bilateral pact between the US Congress and Puerto Rico during which commonwealth was created and, if there was one, such an agreement could not bind any future US Congress"* (Rep. Dan Burton; public hearings held on March 23, 1996, in San Juan, PR).

10. *"The Congress of the United States of America, and not the political parties in Puerto Rico, has the only*

authority to define commonwealth" (Rep. Dan Burton; public hearings held on March 23, 1996, in San Juan, PR).

11. *"Puerto Rico can maintain both English and Spanish as the two official languages as the fifty-first. state, just like Hawaii has two official languages"* (Rep. Abercrombie; public hearings held on March 23, 1996, in San Juan, PR).

Based on the foregoing quotes, it would appear that finally, after many years, the US Congress was addressing the issue of Puerto Rico's status. But for the first time, the people of Puerto Rico were— to their great surprise—being told that there was no bilateral pact between Puerto Rico and the US.

Nothing could be further from the truth.

Back between 1950 and 1952, the first elected governor of Puerto Rico, Muñoz Marín, and his contemporaries had very similar discussions with the US Congress. As a matter of fact, those discussions were so similar to what went on in early 1996 that it felt like deja vu.

Mr. Muñoz complained vigorously that the commonwealth created by the US Congress was just another form of colonial status in which the only freedom the colony had was to elect its own governor. Even the Puerto Rico constitution had to be approved by the US Congress.

And, of course, even back in 1950-52 there was never mention of any kind of bilateral pact between the US and Puerto Rico. Here are some of those quotes from those discussions:

1. *"This bill does not change the fundamental relationship of an unincorporated territory which status Puerto Rico has right now…it is only one step in the process of achieving self-government within an unincorporated territory of the United States, which virtually does not change the relationship with the US"* (Hon. Luis Muñoz Marín, March 14, 1950, referring to H.R. 7674 which became PL

600 which gave the people of Puerto Rico the right to elect their own governor and to write their own, limited, constitution to be approved by US Congress. Public hearings held by the Public Lands Committee of the US House of Representatives during the 81ˢᵗ Congress).

2. *"As already pointed out, H.R. 7674 would not change the status of the island of Puerto Rico relative to the United States"* (Hon. Antonio Fernós-lsern, Resident Commissioner from Puerto Rico, sometime in 1950).

3. *"A commonwealth which under the proposed Constitution seems to be a mere colonialism"* (Rep. Homer H. Budge from Idaho, May 13, 1952).

4. *"Under the Organic Act now in effect if is clear that Congress retains full power to amend or repeal that act. The delegation of authority for local self-government is clearly revocable"* (Rep. George Meader of Michigan, Congressional Record, May 28, 1952).

5. *"The bill under consideration does not change Puerto Rico's political, social and economic relationship with the United States"* (Hon. Oscar L. Chapman, Secretary of the Interior, hearing before the committee on Public Lands relating to S. 3336 which was the Senate version of H.R. 7674).

6. *"And the people of Puerto Rico are still definitely tied in under the supervision of the Congress and under the protection of the provisions of the Federal Relations Act"* (Rep. Crawford of Michigan, May 28, 1952).

III. H.R. 3024 and S. 2019: The Puerto Rico Self-Determination Act
(Introduced in the House of Representatives During the 104th Congress)

Back between 1950 and 1952, while US Congress was debating H.R. 7674 and S. 3336, which were the House and Senate bills that paved the way for Puerto Rico to elect its own governor and write its own limited constitution (which had to be approved by Congress), **Governor Muñoz Marín and Resident Commissioner Fernós-lsern**—along with many other members of Congress and the Administration—went on record to say that **commonwealth, as defined by those congressional bills that created it, was no more than window dressing for the same type of colony that existed prior to 1950.**

Before Rep. Reed Budge of Idaho called the commonwealth a colony on May 13, 1952: *"A better approach might have been to have the people of Puerto Rico write their own constitution without limitations and looking toward either independence, or at least, incorporation in the US in a higher plane than that of a commonwealth."*

Well, this was exactly what Rep. Don Young of Alaska did— along with sixty-four other members of the House of Representatives, both Democrats as well as Republicans (including Rep. Newt Gingrich, the Speaker of the House, Rep. José E. Serrano, Rep. Bill Richardson, and Rep. Kennedy)—when they sponsored H.R. 3024.

And it was exactly what Senator Craig of Idaho did when he— along with six other sponsors, both Democrats and Republicans (including Sen. Paul Simon, Sen. Harry Reid, Sen. Daniel K. Akaka, Sen. Lindsey Graham, Sen. William Cohen, and Sen. Kevin Thomas)—sponsored and introduced S. 2019 in the US Senate.

What they did, perhaps without knowing so, was to take the May 13, 1952, words of Rep. Budge—along with those of Governor Muñoz Marín, Commissioner Fernós-lsern, and members of US

Congress back in the 1950s—and tried to translate them into congressional action in the 1990s. Their goal, after almost one hundred years of colonization, was to help move Puerto Rico toward true self-government.

Based on the words of Governor Muñoz Marín, this was exactly what he attempted to accomplish for Puerto Rico beginning in 1948. But somehow, the only thing that he really got from Congress was the right to be elected governor of a US colony. Fortunately, he was smart enough not to reject Congress's first offer. He accepted the commonwealth legislation given to him in the spirit of compromise and with the promise that it was only the first step on the road to self-government for Puerto Rico.

His comments, when he was handed PL 600 were: *"You know, of course, if the people of Puerto Rico should go crazy, Congress can always get around and legislate again. But I am confident that the Puerto Ricans will not do that and invite congressional legislation that would take back something that was given to the people of Puerto Rico as good United States citizens."*

In my opinion, if Governor Muñoz Marín were alive today, he would be congratulating both Rep. Don Young and Sen. Larry Craig and the other cosponsors of H.R. 3024 and S. 2019, which finally—after so many years of debate—offered Puerto Rico a real opportunity for self-government.

These bills, both the House and the Senate versions, would have done for Puerto Rico what H.R. 7674 and S. 3336 never dared during the age of McCarthyism and Cold War paranoia in America. H.R. 3024 and S. 2019 would have finally given the people of Puerto Rico the right to make their own decisions about their own destiny.

Remembering the words of Governor *Muñoz Marín*, back on March 14, 1950, when he was referring to H.R. 7624, which created the current commonwealth: *"This bill does not change the fundamental status of an unincorporated territory, which Puerto Rico has right now."*

If he had the chance to read both H.R. 3024 and S. 2019, he would have eliminated the word "not" in the above statement and pushed with great vigor the passage of those bills today. In so doing, he would have prevented Puerto Rico from once again becoming the "Poorhouse of the Caribbean" as it was before 1950.

H.R. 3024 passed both the House Subcommittee on Resources and the full committee with a unanimous and a fully bipartisan vote, and no amendments. It was referred to the Rules Committee to be brought out in front of the full House for a debate and a vote.

But there were certain groups that wanted to see the bill derailed because they preferred colonialism over Puerto Rican self-government for very personal and in some instances financial reasons.

The overwhelming bipartisan support this bill enjoyed both in Congress and in Puerto Rico was a testament to the fact that Puerto Rico's time for self-government had finally come. But, unfortunately, H.R. 3024 never made it to the House floor in 1996.

The message from the 1950s still rang true in the 1990s: Puerto Rico was only a US colony subject to the territorial clause, which meant the people of Puerto Rico couldn't even go to the bathroom without permission from the US Congress.

If any local politician tried to convince his or her constituents of anything different, they were only justifying their political existence at great expense to Puerto Rico's economy and people. The time has finally come for Puerto Rico to shake off its colonial shackles and join the rest of the world as either a state of the union or a sovereign nation.

IV. The Economics of Puerto Rico's Political Status

I went into a lot of detail about the effect of federal benefits on Puerto Rico's economy in the first section of *Puerto Rico at the Crossroads*. But the reality, in a nutshell, is this: Unless we contribute to the US federal Treasury and have some clout in Congress as a state, with voting senators and congressmen, Puerto Rico will always be the last in line to receive federal money.

Why? Because the fifty governors of the fifty states will always ask: "Why am I getting less money for my state when our taxpayers pay into the Treasury, while Puerto Rico gets a free ride, without a dime of federal taxes to offset the benefits they will receive? Why should Puerto Rico get any federal funds if it doesn't pay its way?"

Prior to Operation Bootstrap (the famous Puerto Rico economic push during the early 1950s), Puerto Rico had the lowest per capita income of any island in the Caribbean. Puerto Rico was poorer than Haiti, poorer than the Dominican Republic, and poorer than Jamaica.

It remained in this miserable condition from 1898 to the early 1950s, even though it was a territory of the US, and even though it had the section 936 tax gimmick (called section 931 back then), and even though all its residents were US citizens, and even though it had all the advantages of free access to the US markets.

The only thing that changed after Operation Bootstrap, was that Governor Muñoz Marín convinced the US Congress and administration to allow Puerto Rico to participate in the federal welfare benefits of President Roosevelt's New Deal.

In those days, Congress was happy to oblige because the US Treasury was running a budget surplus and America wanted a shiny economic example to keep communism out of the Caribbean during the Cold War.

But what really built-up Puerto Rico's economy was Castro's takeover of Cuba, and the consequent US embargo of Cuba in 1960. This changed the US investment focus from Cuba to Puerto Rico and brought a couple of hundred thousand Cuban refugees to Puerto Rico who brought millions of dollars of their capital and their productive energy to the island.

Today, Americans think that the US no longer needs a shining star in the Caribbean because the Cold War is over, and Cuba is opening up. Well, think again! China today pretty much controls the rest of the Caribbean and Puerto Rico is truly America's last fortress in the region. Without statehood or sovereignty with a free association agreement with the US to keep China out of Puerto Rico, China will have free reign in the entire Caribbean region, just like it does in the South China Sea.

Perhaps Puerto Rico would be better off economically if it were an independent republic, able to make its own treaties with other countries and drive its own economic policy. As a territory, or colony, it has its hands tied in terms of shaping its own future. If Puerto Rico were able to build a viable economic machine, it could become another Singapore, where residents enjoy a very high per capita income.

On the other hand, if Puerto Rico became a state, not only would US federal benefits continue, but Puerto Rico could attract a huge flow of investment capital once again. Leading to an economic boom that would rival the one the island enjoyed in the 1960s. Just like statehood brought prosperity to Hawaii and Alaska, it would do so for Puerto Rico in spades.

However, if Puerto Rico continues as a territory, its fragile economy will continue to sink, turning it back into the "Poorhouse of the Caribbean" that it was during its first fifty years of US territorial status.

Since I do not have emotional or patriotic ties to Puerto Rico's independence, I would much rather see Puerto Rico enjoy its prosperity as the fifty-first state of the union. To me, that is about as sure a bet on economic stability as you can get.

On the other hand, if the people of Puerto Rico choose independence, I would happily continue to live here, knowing that our economy would prosper.

But if Puerto Rico decides to continue on this self-destructive path of insisting on remaining a colony of the US, which I believe will eventually lead it right back into economic ruin, I will be out of here in a flash.

Whatever the outcome is, if you have an economic stake in Puerto Rico, you need to prepare.

If the mood is toward statehood, prepare to invest so that you can make a fortune. If the mood is toward independence, hold on to your money temporarily, and when the smoke clears, invest in Puerto Rico with confidence.

But if there is continued indecision regarding Puerto Rico's status, and it remains stuck in a colonial mentality, then grab your money while you can and run for the hills.

SUPPLEMENT

LETTER SIGNED BY THE FOUR COMMITTEE CHAIRS WITH JURISDICTION OVER PUERTO RICO

U.S. House of Representatives
Committee on Resources
Washington, DC 20515

February 29, 1996

The Honorable Roberto Rexach-Benitez
President of the Senate
The Honorable Zaida Hernández-Torres
Speaker of the House
of the Commonwealth of Puerto Rico
San Juan, Puerto Rico 00901

Dear Mr. Rexach-Benitez and Ms. Hernández-Torres:

The Committee on Resources and the Committee on International Relations are working cooperatively to establish an official record which we believe will enable the House to address the subject-matter of Concurrent Resolution 62, adopted by the Legislature of Puerto Rico on December 14, 1994. While the specific measures addressing Puerto Rico's status which the 104th Congress will consider are still being developed, we believe the history of the self-determination process in Puerto Rico, as well as the record of the Joint Hearing conducted on October 17, 1995 by the Subcommittee on Native American and Insular Affairs and the Subcommittee on Western Hemisphere, lead to the following conclusions with respect to the plebiscite conducted in Puerto Rico on November 14, 1993.

1. The plebiscite was conducted under local law by local authorities, and the voting process appears to have been orderly and consistent with recognized standards for lawful and democratic elections. This locally organized self-determination process was undertaken within the authority of the constitutional government of Puerto Rico, and is consistent with the right of the people of Puerto Rico freely to express their wishes regarding their political status and the form of government under

which they live. The United States recognizes the right of the people of Puerto Rico to self-determination, including the right to approve any permanent political status which will be established upon termination of the current unincorporated territory status. Congress will take cognizance of the 1993 plebiscite results in determining future Federal policy toward Puerto Rico.

2. The content of each of the three status options on the ballot was determined by the three major political parties in Puerto Rico identified with those options, respectively. The U.S. Congress did not adopt a formal position as to the feasibility of any of the options prior to presentation to the voters. Consequently, the results of the vote necessarily must be viewed as an expression of the preferences of those who voted as between the proposals and advocacy of the three major politcal parties for the status option espoused by each such party.

3. None of the status options presented on the ballot received a majority of the votes cast. While the commonwealth option on the ballot received a plurality of votes, this result is difficult to interpret because that option contained proposals to profoundly change rather than continue the current Commonwealth of Puerto Rico government structure. Certain elements of the commonwealth option, including permanent union with the United States and guaranteed U.S. citizenship, can only be achieved through full integration into the U.S. leading to statehood. Other elements of the commonwealth option on the ballot, including a government-to-government bilateral pact which cannot be altered, either are not possible or could only be partially accomplished through treaty arrangements based on separate sovereignty. While the statehood and independence options are more clearly defined, neither of these options can be fully understood on the merits, unless viewed in the context of clear Congressional policy regarding the terms under which either option could be implemented if approved in a future plebiscite recognized by the federal government. Thus, there is a need for Congress to define the real options for change and the true legal and political nature of the status quo, so that the people can know what the actual choices will be in the future.

4. Although there is a history of confusion and ambiguity on the part of some in the U.S. añd Puerto Rico regarding the legal an political nature of the current "commonwealth" local government structure and territorial status, it is incontrovertible that Puerto Rico's present status is that of an unincorporated territory subject in all respects to the authority of the United States Congress under the Territorial Clause of the U.S. Constitution. As such, the current status does not provide guaranteed permanent union or guaranteed citizenship to the inhabitants of the territory of Puerto Rico, nor does the current status provide the basis for recognition of a separate Puerto Rican sovereignty or a binding government-to-government status pact.

5. In light of the foregoing, the results the November 14, 1993 vote indicates that it is the preference of those who cast ballots to change the present impermanent status

in favor of a permanent political status based on full self-government. The only options for a permanent and fully self-governing status are: 1) separate sovereignty and full national independence, 2) separate sovereignty in free association with the United States; 3) full integration into the United States political system ending unincorporated territory status and leading to statehood.

6. Because each ballot option in the 1993 plebiscite addressed citizenship, we want to clarify this issue. First, under separate sovereignty Puerto Ricans will have their own nationality and citizenship. The U.S. political status, nationality, and citizenship provided by Congress under statues implementing the Treaty of Paris during the unincorporated territory period will be replaced by the new Puerto Rican nationhood and citizenship status that comes with separate sovereignty. To prevent hardship or unfairness in individual cases, the U.S. Congress may determine the requirements for eligible persons to continue U.S. nationality and citizenship, or be naturalized, and this will be governed by U.S. law, not Puerto Rican law. If the voters freely choose separate sovereignty, only those born in Puerto Rico who have acquired U.S. citizenship on some other legal basis outside the scope of the Treaty of Paris citizenship statutes enacted by Congress during the territorial period will not be affected. Thus, the automatic combined Puerto Rican and U.S. citizenship described under the definition of independence on the 1993 plebiscite ballot was a proposal which is misleading and inconsistent with the fundamental principles of separate nationality and non-interference by two sovereign countries in each other's internal affairs, which includes regulation of citizenship. Under statehood, guaranteed equal U.S. citizenship status will become a permanent right. Under the present Commonwealth of Puerto Rico government structure, the current limited U.S. citizenship status and rights will be continued under Federal law enacted under the Territorial Clause and the Treaty of Paris, protected to the extent of partial applicaiton of the U.S. Constitution

7. The alternative to full integration into the United States or a status based on separate sovereignty is continuation of the current unincorporate territory status. In that event, the present status quo, including the Commonwealth of Puerto Rico structure for local self-government, presumably could continue for some period of time, until Congress in its discretion otherwise determines the permanent disposition of the territory of Puerto Rico and the status of its inhabitants through the exercise of its authority under the Territorial Clause and the provisions of the Treaty of Paris. Congress may consider proposals regarding changes in the current local government structure, including those set forth in the "Definition of Commonwealth" on the 1993 plebiscite ballot. However, in our view serious consideration of proposals for equal treatment for residents of Puerto Rico under Federal programs will not be provided unless there is an end to certain exemptions from federal tax laws and other non-taxation in Puerto Rico, so that individuals and corporations in Puerto Rico have the same responsibilities and obligations in this regard as the states. Since the "common-

wealth" option on the 1993 plebiscite ballot called for "fiscal autonomy," which is understood to mean, among other things, continuation of the current exemptions from federal taxation for the territory, this constitutes another major politcal, legal and economic obstacle to implementing the changes in Federal law and policy required to fulfill the terms of the "Definition of Commonwealth."

8. In addition, it is important to recognize that the existing Commonwealth of Puerto Rico structure for local self-government, and any other measures which Congress may approve while Puerto Rico remains an unincorporated territory, are not unalterable in a sense that is constitutionally binding upon a future Congress. Any provision, agreement or pact to the contrary is legally unenforceable. Thus, the current Federal laws and policies applicable to Puerto Rico are not unalterable, nor can they be made unalterable, and the current status of the inhabitants is not irrevocable, as proposed under the "commonwealth" option on the 1993 plebiscite ballot. Congress will continue to respect the principle of self-determination in its exercise of Territorial Clause powers, but that authority must be exercised within the framework of the U.S. Constitution and in a manner deemed by Congress to best serve the U.S. national interest. In our view, promoting the goal of full self-government of the people of Puerto Rico, rather than remaing in a separate and unequal status, is in the best interests of the United States. This is particularly true due to the large population of Puerto Rico, the approach of a new century in which a protracted status debate will interfere with Puerto Rico's economic and social development, and the domestic and international interest in determining a path to full self-government for all territories with a colonial history before the end of this century.

9. The record of the October 17,1995 hearing referred to above makes it clear that the realities regarding constitutional, legal and political obstacles to implementing the changes required to fulfill the core elements of the "commonwealth" option on the ballot were not made clear and understandable in the public discussion and political debate leading up to the vote. Consequently, Congress must determine what steps the Federal government should take in order to help move the self-determination process to the next stage, so that the political status aspirations of the people can be ascertained through a truly informed vote in which the wishes of the people are freely expressed within a framework approved by Congress. Only through such a process will Congress then have a clear basis for determining and resolving the question of Puerto Rico's future political status in a manner consistent with the national interest.

Ultimately, Congress alone can determine Federal policy with respect to self-government and self-determination for the residents of Puerto Rico. It will not be possible for the local government or the people to advance further in the self-determination process until the U.S. Congress meets its moral and governmental responsibility to clarify Federal requirements regarding termination of the present unincorporated territory status of Puerto Rico in favor of one of the options for full self-government.

The results of the locally administered 1993 vote are useful in this regard, but in our view are not definitive beyond what has been stated above. The question of Puerto Rico's political status remains open and unresolved.

Sincerely,

Don Young
Chairman
Committee on Resources

Ben Gilman
Chairman
Committee on Intyernational
   Relations

Elton Gallegly
Chairman
Subcommittee on Native American
   and Insular Affairs

Dan Burton
Chairman
Subcommittee on the Western
   Hemisphere

cc: Hon. Héctor Luis Acevedo
     Hon. Rubén Berríos
     Hon. Pedro Rosselló

LETTER SIGNED BY THE DEMOCRATIC LEADERSHIP SUPPORTING H.R. 3024

Congress of the United States
Washington, DC 20515

June 28, 1996

Senator Charlie Rodriguez
Majority Leader, Puerto Rico Senate
The Capitol
San Juan, Puerto Rico 00901

Dear Senator Rodriguez,

As the senior democrats on the House Resources and International Relations Committees we have always been concerned about the economic and political future of Puerto Rico. As the 104th Congress considers proposed legislation regarding the process of self-determination for Puerto Rico, we believe that it is time to reexamine the status issue in light of the 1993 plebiscite.

On December 14, 1994 the Legislature of Puerto Rico adopted Concurrent Resolution 62 which sought congressional guidance regarding the results of the 1993 status plebiscite. Recently, the Chairmen of the relevant committees and subcommittees that deal with Puerto Rico's political status responded to this important resolution. Although we agree with many portions of the letter, we would like to outline some of our views on the issue as well.

We believe that the definition of Commonwealth on the 1993 plebiscite ballot was difficult given Constitutional, and current fiscal and political limitations. Through numerous Supreme Court and other Federal Court decisions, it is clear that Puerto Rico remains an unincorporated territory and is subject to the authority of Congress under the territorial clause. Another aspect of this definition called for the granting of additional tax breaks to Section 936 companies and an increase in federal benefits in order ot achieve parity with all the states without having to pay federal taxes. It is important that any judgement on the future of Puerto Rico be based on sound options that reflect the current budgetary context in the United States. This context should also reflect the bi-partisan agreement being worked on by Congress which reduces Section 936 benefits.

Since Congress has neither approved nor resolved the 1993 plebiscite results, we are in favor of legislation that will establish a future process of self-determination for the people of Puerto Rico. This legislation should include a requirement for status plebiscites to take place within a certain number of years and define various status options in a realistic manner.

In two years, Puerto Rico will celebrate its 100th year as part of the United States. Congress has both a political and moral responsibility to ensure that the 3.5 million Americans living in Puerto Rico have a right to express their views on the important issue of political status on a regular basis.

We hope this additional response to Concurrent Resolution 62 is helpful.

Sincerely,

ROBERT TORRICELLI
Member of Congress

LEE HAMILTON
Member of Congress

BILL RICHARDSON
Member of Congress

DALE KILDEE
Member of Congress

SUMMARY OF THE BILLS PROVIDING FOR PUERTO RICO'S SELF-DETERMINATION PROCESS

105th in Congress

H.R. 856 and S. 472
(Formerly H.R. 3024 and S. 2019)
During 104th Congress

H.R. 856 and S. 472
(Formerly H.R. 3024 and S. 2019 in 104th Congress)

H.R. 856 and S. 472 were bills introduced in the US House of Representatives by Rep. Don Young and in the Senate by Sen. Larry Craig.

The purpose of these two bills was to provide a mechanism that would allow the people of Puerto Rico to resolve their territory (colony) status through a series of referendums that would establish a process that would lead to Puerto Rico achieving full self-government. Though neither of these bills became law, they offer an opportunity to review the alternatives and the process.

Available Alternatives to These Pieces of Legislation

1. **INDEPENDENCE:** The alternative elected by Cuba in 1902 and the Philippines in 1946 after having been US territories since 1898.

2. **FREELY ASSOCIATED STATE OR ASSOCIATED REPUBLIC:** A true commonwealth, which is the alternative chosen by Micronesia and the Marshall Islands in 1986 and 1989.

3. **STATEHOOD:** The alternative chosen by Alaska and Hawaii in 1959.

4. **CONTINUATION OF THE CURRENT STATUS AS AN UNINCORPORATED TERRITORY OF THE US (COLONY):** Puerto Rico has had territory (colony) status since 1898.

The Process

1. THE DECISION PROCESS

A referendum was held prior to December 31, 1998, in which the people of Puerto Rico would decide whether they wanted a change of status or whether would prefer to remain a territory (colony).

If they chose to remain a territory (colony), then they would be given the opportunity to make that choice again in ten years. If they opted for a change in status, then they could vote for either a transition toward sovereignty or a transition toward statehood.

2. THE TRANSITION PROCESS

If the people of Puerto Rico opted for change, then the president of the United States would, within 180 days of that decision, submit to Congress a detailed transition plan showing how Puerto Rico would transition from territory (colony) status to the new status.

The people of Puerto Rico would vote in a second referendum that would give them the opportunity to either accept or reject the transition plan proposed by the president and approved by Congress.

If the people of Puerto Rico rejected the transition plan, they would remain a territory (colony), but would have an opportunity to vote again on whether they wanted a change in status in ten years.

3. THE IMPLEMENTATION PROCESS

If the people of Puerto Rico approved the transition plan, then the president would submit to Congress an implementation plan for the chosen status. The people of Puerto Rico would once again have a referendum either approving or rejecting the implementation plan approved by Congress.

If the people of Puerto Rico rejected the implementation plan, then Puerto Rico would remain a territory (colony) until given another opportunity to vote for change, which would be ten years later.

If they accepted the implementation plan in the final referendum, then Puerto Rico's transition to the new status would be implemented.

4. CITIZENSHIP

One of the key issues at stake for the people of Puerto Rico has always been US citizenship.

Both the House and the Senate version of the bills provided citizenship if the people of Puerto Rico chose either independence or free association. That is, either option to make Puerto Rico a sovereign nation allowed current US citizens who are residents of Puerto Rico to keep their US citizenship for the rest of their lives. However, if these people chose to become Puerto Rican citizens, they would lose their US citizenship. All children born in Puerto Rico to Puerto-Rico-born US citizens would automatically become citizens of Puerto Rico, not US citizens.

In summary, the people of Puerto Rico would vote in three referendums:

1. **FIRST REFERENDUM:** It would still have three choices:
   a. **STATEHOOD**
   b. **SEPARATE SOVEREIGNTY**
   c. **NO CHANGE**

2. **SECOND REFERENDUM:** The second referendum would be to either approve or reject the transition plan for the status selected by the people of Puerto Rico in the first referendum—and submitted by the president and approved by Congress. If this transition plan were to be rejected, then Puerto Rico would remain a territory (colony) until the next opportunity to vote, which would be four years later.

3. **THIRD REFENDUM:** The third referendum would be to either approve or reject the implementation plan for the status selected by the people of Puerto Rico in the first referendum—and submitted by the president and approved by Congress. If the implementation plan were to be rejected, then Puerto Rico would remain a territory (colony) until the next referendum on status, which would be four years later.

Puerto Rico Self-Determinitation Voting Process

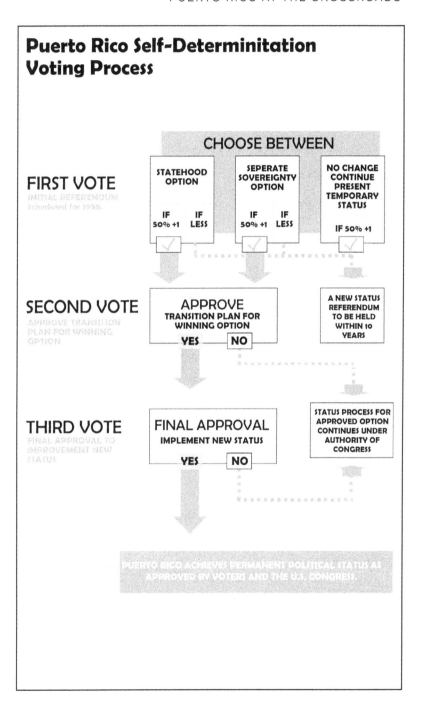

CHOOSE BETWEEN

FIRST VOTE
INITIAL REFERENDUM
Scheduled for 1998.

| STATEHOOD OPTION | SEPERATE SOVEREIGNTY OPTION | NO CHANGE CONTINUE PRESENT TEMPORARY STATUS |

IF 50% +1   IF LESS   IF 50% +1   IF LESS   IF 50% +1

SECOND VOTE
APPROVE TRANSITION
PLAN FOR WINNING
OPTION

APPROVE
TRANSITION PLAN FOR
WINNING OPTION
YES   NO

A NEW STATUS
REFERENDUM
TO BE HELD
WITHIN 10
YEARS

THIRD VOTE
FINAL APPROVAL TO
IMPROVEMENT NEW
STATUS

FINAL APPROVAL
IMPLEMENT NEW STATUS
YES   NO

STATUS PROCESS FOR
APPROVED OPTION
CONTINUES UNDER
AUTHORITY OF
CONGRESS

PUERTO RICO ACHIEVES PERMANENT POLITICAL STATUS AS
APPROVED BY VOTERS AND THE U.S. CONGRESS.

Puerto Rican Change to Permanent Political Status

FIRST VOTE

Voters choose among three options: statehood, seperate soverignty, or a continuation of the present status.

If either the "statehood" or "seperate soverignty" options is chosen by a majority of total votes cast (50%+ 1), the President of the Unites States develops a plan for Puerto Rico to transition to the winning option.

A new status referendum would be held at least once every 10 years if no option wins a majority or if the "no change" option wins a majority of total votes cast.

Presidential Plans
180 Days

Within 180 days of a vote for change to permanent status, a transition plan leading to statehood or seperate soverignty is prepared by the President and submitted to voters within 180 days.

Congressional Action on Plan
180 Days

Congress implements "fast track" procedure for approval of transition plan, which is then submitted to the voters within 180 days.

SECOND VOTE

Electorate approves or rejects the transition plan.

In case of seperate soverignty option, Puerto Ricans can chose between simple independence or independence with free association treaty.

Transition/Implementation Plans

THIRD VOTE

If transition or implementation plans are rejected by voters, process to implement approved option continues under authority of Congress.

If plans are ratified by voters, winning status option is implemented as approved.

FOR

A. STATEHOOD FOR PUERTO RICO
Full integration into the U.S. Constitutional System on the basis of equality.

OR

B. SEPARATE SOVEREIGNTY FOR PUERTO RICO
1. ASSOCIATED REPUBLIC STATUS
Seperate nationhood, negotiated Treaty of Free Association with U.S. under International Law.

2. INDEPENDeNCE
Seperate nationhood. Relations with all nations under applicable International Law and Treaties.

If No Permanent Option Wins a Majority on 1st Vote

TEMPORARY STATUS QUO

If no local option wins a majority or if the status quo option recieves a majority, Puerto Rico remains a locally self-governing "unincorporated territory" of the United States, subject to the discretion of the U.S. Congress under Territorial Clause.

A referendum will be held at least once every 10 years to permit Puerto Rico to choose a course of action leading to permanent soverignty.

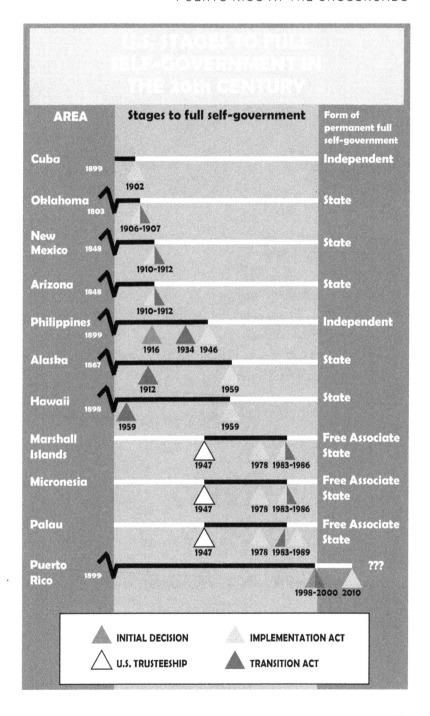

U.S. STAGES TO FULL SELF-GOVERNMENT IN THE 20th CENTURY

AREA	Stages to full self-government	Form of permanent full self-government
Cuba 1899	▬	Independent
Oklahoma 1803	1902	State
New Mexico 1848	1906-1907	State
Arizona 1848	1910-1912	State
Philippines 1899	1910-1912	Independent
Alaska 1867	1916 1934 1946	State
Hawaii 1898	1912 1959	State
Marshall Islands	1959 1959	Free Associate State
Micronesia	1947 1978 1983-1986	Free Associate State
Palau	1947 1978 1983-1986	Free Associate State
Puerto Rico 1899	1947 1978 1983-1989 1998-2000 2010	???

INITIAL DECISION   IMPLEMENTATION ACT
U.S. TRUSTEESHIP   TRANSITION ACT

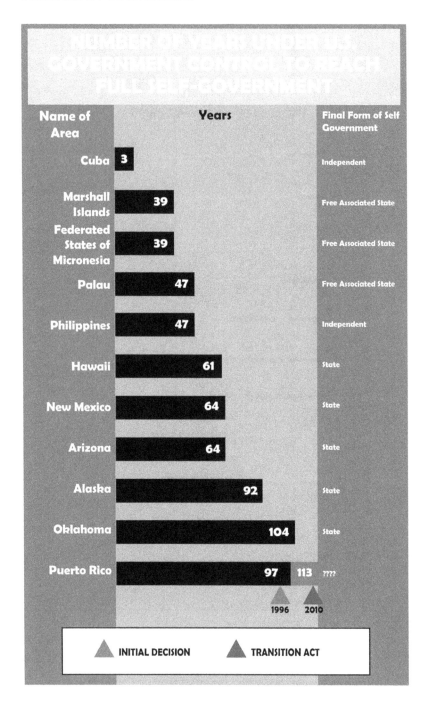

NUMBER OF YEARS UNDER U.S. GOVERNMENT CONTROL TO REACH FULL SELF-GOVERNMENT

Name of Area	Years	Final Form of Self Government
Cuba	3	Independent
Marshall Islands	39	Free Associated State
Federated States of Micronesia	39	Free Associated State
Palau	47	Free Associated State
Philippines	47	Independent
Hawaii	61	State
New Mexico	64	State
Arizona	64	State
Alaska	92	State
Oklahoma	104	State
Puerto Rico	97 / 113	????

1996 2010

▲ INITIAL DECISION   ▲ TRANSITION ACT

THE FINAL CHAPTER

What Destroyed the Young Bill?

Despite strong support, the roof caved in on H.R. 856, known as the Young Bill, for many reasons. Both House Speaker Rep. Newt Gingrich and Minority Leader Rep. Andrew Gephardt cosponsored the bill, which had almost one hundred cosponsors—both Democrats and Republicans.

It passed the House Resources committee twice with only one out of forty-one votes against it.

The issues dealing with "fairness" to the opposing party in Puerto Rico, the PDP—which were the main concern of Rep. George Miller, the ranking member of the committee—were addressed, settled, and incorporated into the bill.

The issue dealing with the use of the English language in Puerto Rico's public schools, which was the main concern of Rep. Gerald Solomon, chairman of the Rules Committee, was also addressed.

The Young Bill was ready to be scheduled for the House floor in October 1997 when things suddenly and surprisingly fell apart.

Was It Racism?

A small group of Republicans, some of whom were alleged to have also rebelled against the speaker and tried to unseat him, launched a vicious campaign to deny the people of Puerto Rico self-determination.

Their excuses for opposing the bill were reflected in manufactured facts, lies, and half-truths that began appearing as full-page advertisements in influential publications on Capitol Hill, those promoted by Puerto Rican special interests. Those advertisements implied that:

1. The Young Bill was not a self-determination bill but a statehood bill.
2. The majority of the people of Puerto Rico were welfare recipients.

3. The people of Puerto Rico did not speak English.
4. If the Young Bill had become law, it would have paved the way for Puerto Rico to become a Spanish-speaking state that would have sent Democrats to Congress and increased the US welfare costs into the billions each year.

The smears in these ads were ugly.

Did a "Bogus" Definition of Commonwealth Prevail?

The main objection to the Young Bill actually came from the PDP, one of the two major local Puerto Rican parties but NOT the party in power at the time.

Referencing the 1993 plebiscite, they claimed that since 48 percent of Puerto Ricans voted for "commonwealth," 46 percent voted for Statehood, and the rest voted for Independence, the results settled the question of what the voters of Puerto Rico would prefer.

The problem with this argument is the "commonwealth" definition used in the 1993 plebiscite was a wish that could never become a reality. It was a definition that the US Congress could never accept because it violated the US Constitution.

To quote Rep. Dan Burton (R), chairman of the House Oversite Committee: "Forty-eight percent of the voters in Puerto Rico in 1993 voted for a bogus definition of commonwealth."

Political parties in Puerto Rico have never been divided by ideological issues like Republicans versus Democrats in the US Instead, they are divided based on the status debate over commonwealth, statehood, or independence. Both Democrats and Republicans are scattered among the two major parties. Thus, if the people of Puerto Rico were to vote against the present status, an entire party apparatus would suddenly be voted out of business. A lot of PDP party hacks and cronies would be out of a job. Motivated by self-preservation rather than what might be best for the people of Puerto Rico and the US taxpayers, the PDP party decided to rig the plebiscite election by inventing a definition of the commonwealth status that, I am sure, every state in the union would give their right arm (and their statehood) to have.

Because the US Congress was not writing the rules of the game (as are spelled out in H.R. 856), each party could actually invent its own definition and place its wish list on the ballot.

It is easy to define statehood or independence. But "commonwealth" was an invented status for this colony, and the commonwealth Party's very existence depends on maintaining this status quo. They dared not spell out a definition that would reflect the current territorial/colonial status, so they decided to make their definition something that they would like to have but did not have at the time.

They defined "commonwealth" as follows:

1. *Permanent relationship with the US (attained through statehood)*
2. *Permanent and guaranteed*
3. *US citizenship (achieved through statehood)*
4. *Continuation of section 936 tax gimmick forever (precludes the US Congress from making a change in the IRS code, which is unconstitutional)*
5. *Full federal benefits (achieved through statehood)*
6. *Full exemption from paying federal taxes (achieved through independence)*
7. *Veto power over laws enacted by the US Congress through a "bilateral pact" (achieved through independence as it would be unconstitutional for a US territory to have this power)*

If this choice were offered to residents of Connecticut or Nebraska or any of the other fifty states, I am sure that 99.9 percent of their voters would vote for it.

Fortunately, most Puerto Rican voters understand realities, and 52 percent voted for a status that was realistic (statehood or independence) and not some pipe dream. Only 48 percent voted for the "free lunch" that could never actually become a reality due to constitutional issues.

But the most significant point of this 1993 plebiscite was the fact that 100 percent of Puerto Rican voters voted for a change in the current status.

But when you place the two definitions of statehood and commonwealth side by side, a second point stands out like a sore thumb. About half the voters voted for statehood that included paying federal taxes and the other half voted for all the benefits that statehood would bring without paying federal taxes. In other words, a "free lunch."

It was clear from this vote that the people of Puerto Rico wanted a change, and that change was for a closer relationship with the US.

What Were the Real Motives?

Based on many internal polls of members of the 105th Congress taken in the summer and fall of 1997, the majority of members, both Democrats and Republicans, with only a few exceptions, were in favor of bringing the Young Bill to a vote in October of 1997.

But perhaps racism, fueled by a very clever and vicious advertising campaign, combined with massive pressure on the Republican leadership by a tiny handful of zealots who felt that adding a Latino state to the union would blemish the racial purity of America, prevailed.

Unfortunately, the Young Bill ran out of time in October of 1997. But hopefully, decency and common sense will prevail, and a new version of the Young Bill will garner support and finally get the attention it deserves.

The Washington Times   WEDNESDAY, SEPTEMBER 24, 1997 / PAGE A5

H.R. 856
The Budget Buster

The Consequences of H.R. 856 are an Expensive Proposition

However, there has been <u>no debate</u> in Congress over the costs

Net Cumulative Cost for U.S. Government

"Estimates show that **statehood would cause an increase** **to Puerto Rico of $3.253 Billion.** Over the full fore... cost to the U.S. Government would be betwe...

<u>Source:</u> 1990 KPMG Peat Marwick Study on the ...ood

Federal Taxes to be C... ...illion
in Puerto Rico ... ...eral Transfers
Even to P... to Puerto Rico

"We e...
who fil...

...EITC
...uerto Rican
...a total of about
...ggregate net tax liability
w... ...h. If the additional EITC that
coul... ...ed by legal nonfilers residents were
about $... ...t, **it would be sufficient to eliminate** the
$49 million of aggregate **net federal income tax liability.**"

<u>Source:</u> 1996 GAO Report on Tax Policy

"Fiscal relations between Puerto Rico
and the Federal Government would change
significantly with any change in status.
Statehood would increase taxes paid,
but this increase **would be more than offset**
by higher federal transfers to
the island residents and governments.
As a result, net transfers (spending less taxes)
to the island would be nearly **$18 billion higher.**"

<u>Source:</u> 1990 Congressional Budget Office
Economic Impact Study on Puerto Rico Status

Are You Willing to Pay this Price?

H.R. 856: MAKING PUERTO RICO OUR 51ST STATE

Paid for by Puerto Rico First, Inc.

MISLEADING BASED ON INCOMPLETE DATA

173

The Excuse Used to Kill H.R. 856

When it comes to Puerto Rico's status change, US legislators have always been concerned about the impact it might have on the federal budget, so the excuse used by a handful of Republicans to kill H.R. 856 in 1997 was that statehood would cost the US too much.

In battling H.R. 856, opponents of Puerto Rico's self-determination cleverly used advertising that contained misleading (and in some instances false) information to influence those members who prided themselves on being fiscally responsible. The ad on page illustrates this point.

If you take a look at the ad, it portrays H.R. 856 as a statehood bill. It then quotes information from the 1996 GAO report on Tax Policy and the 1990 CBO report that appears to show the cost to the federal Treasury should Puerto Rico become a state. But the ad does not say that this information was taken out of context and that the studies were done based on incomplete and in some instances non-applicable information and assumptions.

For example, the CBO experiment was conducted primarily based on the removal of section 936 and changes in federal transfers. It did not consider the unique sectoral composition of Puerto Rico's economy, including income expenditure relationships and flexibility of prices as a more realistic Computable General Equilibrium model might between sectors. And it did not account for the fact that Puerto Rico's economy as a colony has been driven by manufacturing that exists based on a tax gimmick, making that segment of the economy disproportionate to one that might have a more solid economic base.

It also totally ignored that with the phaseout of section 936 and the advent of statehood, other internal programs implemented locally, and natural efficiencies would occur that would stimulate the economy, which I discussed at some length in the first section of this booklet.

But the most important points that both these studies missed were the fact that with statehood, the cost to the federal Treasury would be reduced by the current cost of section 936 tax credits, and that statehood would stimulate both internal and external investment, which would accelerate faster economic growth.

With the accelerated increase of per capita income in Puerto Rico as a result of statehood and the economic stimulus that it represents, the 1996 GAO report on Tax Policy would then have to be updated to reflect a surplus of tax revenues rather than a cost of earned income tax credits.

When these factors are accounted for, the change of status from colony to statehood would create a surplus of income to the federal Treasury rather than a drain as the misleading advertising tried to portray. The next few pages will show the real numbers.

Commonwealth Is Not Representative Democracy

In the first section of this booklet, I went into considerable depth as to the impact and the influence that US corporations operating under section 936 exerted on both the economic and political scene in Puerto Rico.

Back in the 1800s and right up until the early 1900s, the coffee and sugar interests controlled all aspects of Puerto Rico's economic and political life. First as a colony of Spain, with emphasis on coffee, and then as a colony of the US, changing the focus to sugar. Puerto Rico's man on the street had to play second fiddle to the deep pocket interests of colonial exploitation. That's why Puerto Rico was the "Poorhouse of the Caribbean" right up to the mid-fifties.

Nothing has changed in a couple hundred years.

Today, just like then, Puerto Rico's economy is still held captive by outside interests and the commonwealth political structure does not facilitate true representative democracy.

On the economic side, the $3.8 billion dollars per year in section 936 tax credits enjoyed by the 936 companies exerted an iron grip on all aspects of local economic life in Puerto Rico until it was phased out. Of this $3.8 billion, the pharmaceutical industry's share was about two-thirds while it employed less than 25,000 workers directly (only 2 percent of the total employment base at the time), many of whom were temporary and part-time employees who didn't get regular corporate fringe benefits.

Even though section 936 was phased out, corporate 936 beneficiaries, especially pharmaceutical companies, use their powerful lobby in Washington to pour millions of dollars annually into maintaining Puerto Rico as a colony to serve the interests of outside investors rather than the people of Puerto Rico. The media are held captive by the advertising dollars spent by these companies. Few media outlets dare utter meaningful criticism of their tax breaks or the current colonial status for fear of getting cut off from this easy money.

Until the colonial yoke can be shaken, political forces supported by these moneyed interests will continue to shape Puerto Rico's future—just as coffee and sugar money ran the island a hundred plus years ago. Sadly, this means that the man on the street will be kept quiet with his/her food-stamp checks and no true voting representation.

That is colonialism! It's fueled by welfare for the poor and tax gimmicks for the rich and it is all financed by interests outside of Puerto Rico.

Real Numbers from History

In order to build a healthy economy, there must be sufficient internal capital. The product of this capital must be reinvested into the local economy. In Puerto Rico, the opposite is true. Outside capital is only invested in order to repatriate the product back in the US.

If we examine the transfers of capital to and from Puerto Rico between 1981 and 1994, we find that more than $2.2 billion left Puerto Rico than came into the island. Phrased another way, Puerto Rico had $12.3 billion of investment come in and $14.5 of investment leave during this thirteen-year period.

The capital that left was mainly 936 corporation repatriation of profits.

You can't build a solid economy when the capital created by the productivity of the workers is shipped out as soon as it is created.

In 1989, the average tax credit per employee enjoyed by 936 corporations was $22,375. That same year, the average annual wage of 936 company employees was $20,540. In other words, 936 companies who operated in Puerto Rico had their workers' salaries paid by the federal government, and then they kept the profits and sent them back to their parent companies while the US taxpayer spent $13 billion to keep Puerto Rico's welfare rolls brimming with giveaways.

What a rip-off for the US taxpayer!

Colonial Status Disguised as a Commonwealth

As of 1995, Puerto Rico's, colonial status was costing US taxpayers close to $13 billion dollars per year. Today, that number is much higher.

Talk about budget busters!

Here is a breakdown of the fiscal 1995 federal payments to Puerto Rico:

Payments to Individuals	*$ 5.0 billion*
Lost tax revenues (tax credits)	*$ 3.8 billion*
Intergovernmental Transfers	*$ 2.4 billion*
Food Stamps	*$ 1.1 billion*
Wages of Fed. Workers	*$ 0.55 billion*
Total	*$12.85 billion*

Under Independence or Free Associated state, Puerto Rico would finally be in a position to create its own treaties with other countries. It would also no longer be burdened with US federal laws that may make it uncompetitive (for example, minimum wage or environmental laws that only very rich countries can afford). Puerto Rico might even become another Singapore, no longer requiring US federal assistance, so the cost to the US within five or ten years could dwindle to zero.

Once again, the problem is "commonwealth" (colony).

Under statehood, Puerto Rico would be paying into the federal Treasury, and its tax-haven status would be out. Here are some numbers crunched by several researchers in Cambridge, Massachusetts, including Dr. Thomas Hexner, Dr. Glenn P. Jenkins, director of the Harvard School of International Law and Taxation and Fellow of the Harvard Institute for International Development, and Dr. Fernando Lefort, Professor of Economics at University of Santiago, Chile.

Transfers to Puerto Rico from federal budget as a result of statehood	*$1.4 billion*
US federal taxes	*-$4.12 billion*
Net profit to US taxpayers the first year of Puerto Rico statehood	*$2.72 billion*

Again, the problem is "commonwealth" (colony).

But that is only half the story.

Here is the other half...

Divergence/Convergence

In the early part of the nineteenth century, there were large disparities between per capita incomes among many states. For example, back in 1929, South Carolina had the per capita income that was 22 percent of New York, which was the richest state at the time. In 1940, Mississippi also had a per capita income that was 22 percent of Delaware, which was the richest at the time. The American Civil War and slavery had done an awesome job of creating and keeping those disparities for a long time.

However, by 1990, South Carolina had a per capita income that was 71 percent, and Mississippi had its per capita income increase to 50 percent of the income of Connecticut, which had become the richest state.

In other words, states converged on each other economically.

But while all this converging has been going on among the fifty states, our little colony in the Caribbean, which supposedly was the "best of both worlds," has been falling behind.

To give credit where it is due, between the years of 1950 and 1975, Puerto Rico did gain some ground in terms of catching up to the fifty US states due to agrarian reform in the 1940s and the push for industrial development with emphasis on outside investment (mainly from the US) driven by tax gimmicks during the 1950s and 1960s.

But over the last twenty years, Puerto Rico's financial wellbeing has fallen behind not just the US but even the rest of the Caribbean.

As of the writing of this pamphlet, Puerto Rico's per capita income stands at around 40 percent of the US average per capita income—as measured against GDP. Between 1955 and 1972, it moved from 22 percent to 45 percent. But in the last few years, Puerto Rico has been regressing.

Here is why.

Between the years 1955 to 1972, the average rate of investment was (as measured against the GDP) at 29.2 percent. Then, between 1973 and 1984, it dropped to 17 percent, and between 1984 and 1994, it went down to 14 percent.

As a result, Puerto Rico's GDP growth rate, which was 5.9 percent between 1955 and 1972 (a healthy rate), went down to 2.1 percent over the last twenty years. Not good!

Yes folks, we've been going backward while the rest of US has been moving forward.

Again, the problem is "commonwealth" status (colony).

What's most embarrassing is that Puerto Rico—once the economic powerhouse of the Caribbean due to flying under the US flag and getting billions in federal welfare funds and tax gimmicks—has a per capita income half that of St. Kitts, a tiny hole-in-the-wall independent banana republic.

How did the "Shining Star of the Caribbean," miss out?

Well, we blindly bought into the propaganda of the big "best of both worlds" lie while colonial status kept our economy from expanding at the kind of pace that some insignificant island banana republics were able to achieve.

But all this can change.

By either becoming an independent republic or a freely associated state, Puerto Rico could become another Singapore OR the fifty-first US state; Puerto Rico would be plugged into all the confidence-driven investment money that comes with statehood.

Based on the study done by Hex Inc., statehood would accelerate Puerto Rico's economic growth by 2.2 percent to 3.5 percent. That study shows that our per capita income would have increased by 20 percent had Puerto Rico become a state in 1995. And at that rate, the island's per capita income would be approaching US averages within twenty years.

Here is a table that the writing of this pamphlet reflects the INCEASE in Puerto Rico's per capita income of $7,296 over the next twenty-seven years using the above assumptions:

Benefits of Statehood (if achieved in 1994) (assuming a convergence rate of 3.5%)	
Year	Change in per capita income under statehood
2000	$1,343.70
2005	$2,641.00
2010	$4,095.70
2020	$5,706.60
2025	$9,405.40

Using Hawaii as an example, the number of firms doing business there increased *sixfold* between 1955 and 1971, and tourism increased *fifteenfold* during this period, a 20 percent per year compounded increase.

So, when fiscally responsible legislators ask themselves: "What is the cost to US taxpayers of Puerto Rico becoming a state?"

The first answer should be: "A heck of a lot less than what it would cost for the US to maintain colonial status."

And just the initial numbers, strictly based on today's realities, prove it. The first year alone would create a $2.72 billion savings.

But when you begin adding the acceleration in our economy as a result of statehood, which would reduce unemployment and reduce the utilization of social benefits combined with accelerating federal tax receipts, the total savings to US taxpayers could easily top $100 billion or more.

From this perspective, the price of Puerto Rico's "commonwealth" (colony) status is indeed prohibitive.

Puerto Rico has been called "The only colony in the history of colonialism that has effectively exploited the colonizer."

A Solid Economic Foundation for Puerto Rico

The Young Bill was the solution and not the problem, as some argued. But since it was killed, it's worth revisiting some of the lessons so we can do better next time.

1. **The Young Bill was not a statehood bill but a true self-determination bill, and that is why even the Puerto Rico Independence Party (which is famous for opposing anything and everything that originates in US Congress) supported it enthusiastically.**

2. **Contrary to the false propaganda that was circulated, Puerto Rican statehood would save US taxpayers $2.72 billion the first year—with more savings to come as the island's economy grows and prospers.**

3. **In the event of statehood, when the congressional districts are set up, those who are currently mayors of local districts will probably carry congressional votes. And many of the mayors are solid Republicans.**

4. **English is not an issue. Prior to 1952, the language of public instruction in Puerto Rico was English. Puerto Rico's first elected governor, Muñoz Marín, passed a law then that made Spanish the language of public instruction, yet he sent his own kids to English speaking private schools. Most Puerto Ricans speak English because it is taught today as a second language in public schools. Most Puerto Ricans have access to Cable TV, which is in English. Puerto Rico, as a state would be no different from Louisiana (French), New Mexico (Spanish), Pennsylvania (Amish Country Dutch and German), or Williamsburg, Brooklyn, a predominantly Hassidic Jewish section where the language of instruction in schools is in Hebrew. Ethnically, Puerto Rico will fit into America. It is a potpourri of cultures and languages**

that coexist within a common bond of freedom, democracy, and free enterprise.

5. Puerto Ricans are decent people who have strong family values. The issues of crime, drugs and welfare are no different from those in any other urban environment. Puerto Rico is a nice place to live, and it could be even better once it is able to shake off the yokes of colonialism that pull it down.

GRAPHS THAT REFLECT PUERTO RICO'S ECONOMIC REALITIES IN LIGHT OF A STATUS CHANGE

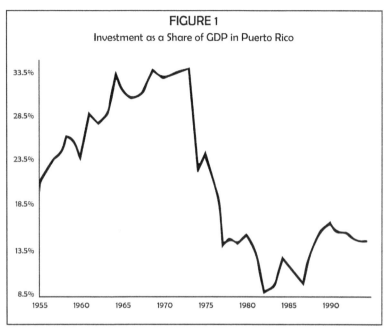

FIGURE 1

Investment as a Share of GDP in Puerto Rico

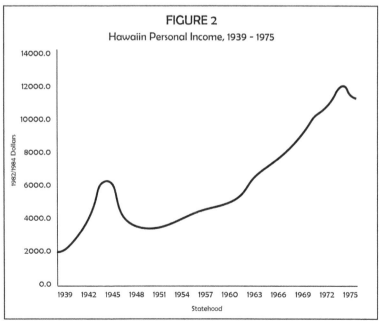

FIGURE 2

Hawaiin Personal Income, 1939 - 1975

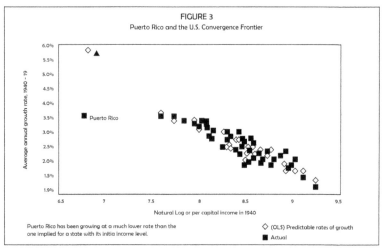

FIGURE 3
Puerto Rico and the U.S. Convergence Frontier

Average annual growth rate, 1940 - 19

Natural Log or per capital income in 1940

Puerto Rico has been growing at a much lower rate than the one implied for a state with its initia income level.

◇ (OLS) Predictable rates of growth
■ Actual

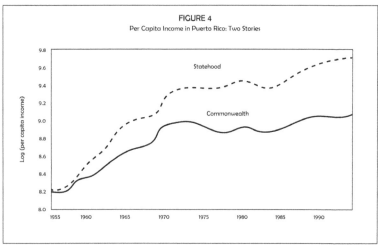

FIGURE 4
Per Capita Income in Puerto Rico: Two Stories

Log (per capita income)

Statehood

Commonwealth

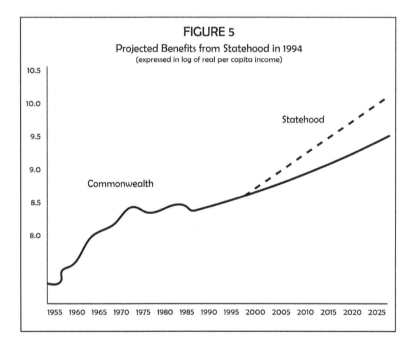

FIGURE 5

Projected Benefits from Statehood in 1994

(expressed in log of real per capita income)

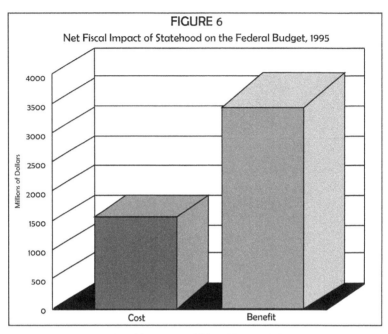

FIGURE 6
Net Fiscal Impact of Statehood on the Federal Budget, 1995

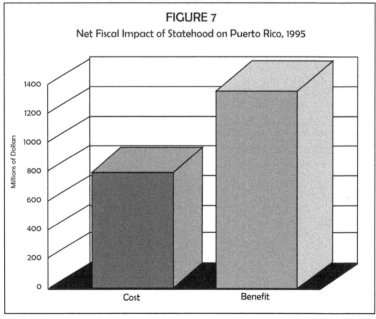

FIGURE 7
Net Fiscal Impact of Statehood on Puerto Rico, 1995

APPENDIX II

ANNEX #1

Elección	Vencedor(a)	Partido	Votos	%	Mayoría	%	Total Votos	Inscritos
1948	Luis Muñoz Marín	PPD	392,386	61.2	209,409	32.6	640,714	873,085
1952	Luis Muñoz Marín	PPD	431,409	64.9	305,181	45.9	664,947	883,219
1956	Luis Muñoz Marín	PPD	435,215	62.5	260,532	37.4	696,574	873,842
1960	Luis Muñoz Marín	PPD	459,759	58.2	206,517	26.2	789,487	941,034
1964	Roberto Sánchez Vilella	PPD	492,531	59.2	204,027	24.5	831,451	1,002,000
1968	**Luis A. Ferré**	**PNP**	**400,815**	**43.6**	**26,775**	**2.9**	**918,829**	**1,176,895**
1972	Rafael Hernández Colón	PPD	658,856	50.7	95,247	7.3	1,299,884	1,555,504
1976	**Carlos Romero Barceló**	**PNP**	**703,968**	**48.3**	**43,567**	**3.0**	**1,458,134**	**1,701,217**
1980	**Carlos Romero Barceló**	**PNP**	**759,926**	**47.2**	**3,037**	**0.2**	**1,609,311**	**2,071,777**
1984	Rafael Hernández Colón	PPD	822,709	47.8	53,750	3.1	1,722,787	1,959,877
1988	Rafael Hernández Colón	PPD	871,858	48.7	51,516	2.9	1,792,153	2,144,583
1992	**Pedro Rosselló**	**PNP**	**938,969**	**49.9**	**75,980**	**4.0**	**1,881,872**	**2,235,625**
1996	**Pedro Rosselló**	**PNP**	**1,006,331**	**51.1**	**130,479**	**6.6**	**1,967,705**	**2,380,676**
2000	Sila María Calderón	PPD	978,860	48.6	59,666	3.0	2,012,135	2,447,032
2004	Aníbal Acevedo Vilá	PPD	963,303	48.4	3,566	0.2	1,990,372	2,440,131
2008	**Luis Fortuño**	**PNP**	**1,025,965**	**52.8**	**224,894**	**11.6**	**1,941,704**	**2,458,036**
2012	Alejandro García Padilla	PPD	896,060	47.7	11,285	0.6	1,877,055	2,402,941
2016	**Ricardo Rosselló Nevares**	**PNP**	**660,510**	**41.8**	**46,320**	**2.9**	**1,580,184**	**2,867,557**

Reference: electionspuertorico.org/referencia/gobernadores.html

Elecciones en Puerto Rico:
Gobernadores de Puerto Rico Electos por Votación Popular
Elecciones Generales de 1948 a 2016

ATTACHMENT A

OUTLINE OF BUSINESS PLAN FOR ACHIEVING STATEHOOD
A. ODISHELIDZE

Where we failed in the past:

1. Our approach was focused strictly on what's right for Puerto Rico and we failed to find the motivating factors that would move Congress in favor of our objective.

2. We did not address main obstacle to statehood which was Sec 933, because many wealthy Puerto Ricans did not want to pay federal taxes, yet claimed to be statehooders and this allowed CFC's to form strong opposition aligned with the PDP

3. Input was discouraged or ignored

4. Statehood was used as a political crutch In order to win elections, which interfered with statehood objectives

5. Allocation of expenses was not strategically implemented

How we might be more effective in the future:

1. Create a core group of a dozen or so individuals who may have the following credentials and pick a three-man rotating board that will make decisions:

    a. Attorneys specializing in:

        i. Election law

        ii. Constitutional law

        iii. Legislative procedures

        iv. Litigation

        v. Corporate law

    b. Experience with lobbying issues and fees charged in that field

    c. Sales/marketing including social media

    d. Corporate senior management

    e. Entrepreneur

    f. Government administration

    g. Legislative administration

    h. Fundraising experience

    i. Academic experience specializing in finance and economics.

2. Set up an agenda/business plan for objectives and ways to meet those objectives with timelines.

3. Hire lobbyists and other experts that will implement that plan.

4. Set up a budget protocol, so that more funds are spent on the most effective areas that produce the best results and minimize the cost of less productive areas.

5. Set up a process so that regular input from everyone is solicited and then use that input for a "Board of Directors"(perhaps three people), who will analyze that input and make a decision for future action.

6. Appoint a professional "Manager" (not practicing Attorney) who will supervise operation based on the objectives determined by the "Board" for each participant.

Belt and Road Caribbean

Nicaragua- The big headline here was an attempted Chinese canal through Lake Nicaragua to circumvent the US dominance of the Panama Canal. The Canal project was to be financed by Chinese Billionaire Wang Jing. The Nicaraguan legislature granted his new canal company a 50 year license to develop the canal in 2013. His company HK Nicaragua Canal Development Company intended to dig and develop the canal. Jing lost significant amounts of money in 2015 and 2016, purportedly bringing his net worth under a billion dollars. This, along with significant developmental barriers brought the project to a halt. The company still holds the 50 Year rights to build the canal. Nicaragua has claimed that they are still doing dry exploring but the project looks to have failed. Nothing concrete has materialized.

Costa Rica- They signed a Cooperation agreement with the Peoples Republic of China in 2018. In the agreement, Costa Rica officially endorsed the belt-and-road initiative. China has been a growing destination for Costa Rican goods. Costa Rica accounts for a large portion of the Central America's foreign investment share at 22% (not just China--all countries). Although the investment hasn't grown dramatically in the last 3 years. In 2017 China offered $130 Million in aid and bought $300 Million in Costa Rican Bonds.

Guatemala- Relations with the US still dominate the economy, and import-export totals for the US are huge. 42% of exports and 40% of imports are with the US. They are not signatories to the belt and road initiative. Foreign direct investment grew in 2019 from $293 Million to $340 Million. The electricity sector had the largest source of investment, China is not a top 5 investing country in the sector but the US is. Guatemala struggles to attract investment because of it's political instability. In 2013 the Chinese Electrical company TEAS expressed interest in investing in Guatemala and selling products there, there has been no update since 2013. Guatemala does not seem like a high priority on the Belt-and-Road. Guatemala still recognizes Taiwan.

Honduras- In a September 2019 interview, the President of Honduras lamented declining US investment under the Trump administration. Honduras still recognizes Taiwan, and the president stated that they are still with Taiwan. Along with Panama, Honduras was the only country in Central America to experience a growth in foreign direct investment last year. Regionally El Salvador has been perhaps the friendliest with the Chinese. The USA dominates export and import in the country with over 30% of the share in both categories.

Panama- Is an official signatory of the Belt-and-Road initiative and moved to only recognize the PRC--they have no informal recognition of the ROC like many other countries. They were the first country in Latin America to join the initiative. The Chinese Company Landbridge Group bought the largest port in Panama. It is in the Colon Free Trade Zone on the Caribbean side of the Panama Canal. The company is state subsidized. A large bridge, the Atlantic Bridge, was recently completed in Colon. The bridge was built by a French company, but designed by US company and the vast Chinese firm China Communication Construction Company(CCCC). The Chinese, under the direction of the CCCC and state owned China Harbor Company Limited are planning to build a fourth bridge spanning the canal, they were authorized by the Panamanian Government in 2018 to build it. The Chinese presented a plan to the president of Panama in early 2019 to build a high speed railway connecting the rest of the country to the canal zone.

This is not a complete list for Panama. The country is heavily infiltrated by the Chinese and there are likely to be more projects there.

Colombia- The nation is the only one in the Andean region that has not joined the Belt and Road initiative and remains isolated in that respect. They have one major project in the country with Chinese investment, a highway called Autopisa del Mar 2. In terms of FDI (Foreign Direct Investment) China lags far behind in Columbia. The United States invested $2.5 Billion in 2018, by contrast the Chinese invested a mere $32 Million. English, Spanish and Panamanian investment all surpassed a Billion. 10 European countries and Canada also surpassed the total invested by China, many by wide margins. Colombia is more focused of on the Venezuela crises, remains in the US orbit, and is weary of the risks of the Belt and Road.

Venezuela- Joined. China has loaned more than $67 billion to Venezuela, and much of it has been repaid with the vast oil reserves in the country. China was integral in financing the rise of Venezuela under Chavez. China and Venezuela entered a strategic partnership in 2001, and a "Comprehensive Strategic Partnership in 2014". China stopped lending in 2016 due to the country's internal chaos and bleak economic outlook. Prior to that the Chinese had invested in over 790 projects in the country. Over the past 11 years China has frozen many investments in the country.

Guyana- In 2018 Joined the belt and road initiative. The Chinese have won several bids in the country including the expansion of the Airport by China Harbor engineering. 7 out of 11 bids on a large bridge in the country were placed by Chinese firms. The Chinese also won the rights to build a large hydroelectric plant in the country. The damn project, like many of the fast and loose belt-and-road projects, has been halted.

Trinidad- This nation has officially joined belt-and-road, all others on this list have signed Bi-lateral Chinese agreements amounting to the BRI but Trinidad and Tobago is a formal member of the initiative. Trinidad have a large share of its economy involved in Petroleum refining. That being said it is small in the scale compared to larger Petroleum producers. The country is among the wealthiest in the Caribbean, but the most corrupt. Strong backlash has been felt in the form of anti-Chinese violence. The National Academy of Performing Arts in the Port-of-Spain has been built by a Chinese firm as well as many other infrastructure projects. The country is ripe for corruption and cushy deals with the Chinese. The PLA has cooperated with the Trinidad and Tobago Defense Force, including several staff visits and a 2014 arms deal. This policy paper uses Trinidad and Tobago as a case study and sites it as being a particularly pervasive example of BRI penetration.

Cuba- Signed an agreement of economic cooperation in 2018. After Venezuela, China is Cuba's second largest trading partner. In the last 18 years, China has written off about $10 Billion in foreign debt, over half of that has been Cuban. From 2008 to 2015 investment in Cuba fell 17% and exports fell 5%. Between 2011 and 2014 four countries: China, Mexico, Japan and Russia wrote off over $40 of losses on Cuba a value of about half it's GDP. Though Cuba's animosity to the US would make it an appealing option to invest in, the weak economy has prevented vast Chinese investment there. Although China is interested in Cuban petroleum and nickel. This National Interest 2018 article states that the lack of economic reforms in Cuba have deterred China and Russia from investing.

Haiti- The country still recognizes Taiwan as the legitimate government of China. It does not have a bilateral agreement with China. In 2017 China formulated and exchanged plans with Haiti to invest over $30 billion into modernizing Port-Au-Prince, including a new power plant, a new city hall and thousands of apartments. The Chinese have pledged investment in Haiti but significant structural barriers remain in Haiti.

Dominican Republic- In 2018 the Dominican Republic signed a bilateral agreement with China and severed relations with Taiwan after 69 years. China pledged $600 million loan to help develop infrastructure and a package that could potentially total more than $3.1 Billion in low-interest loans. It is purported that China is very interested in the ports of the country as well as a Haiti-DR railroad. They could invest as much as $2 billion in free trade areas to bonify trade.

PR- See other documents.

In terms of the EB-5 visa program, Puerto Rico is an attractive option and many articles espouse this view because the investment requirements are lower and Puerto Rico possesses an attractive tax code loopholes. There are very few articles and essentially one project that is listed with any consistency. It is the Four Seasons Cayo Largo in PR. This article discusses it and the program. The story is about an Indian investor, not a Chinese investor, investing in Cayo Largo. The story does note that the largest group of applicants are the Chinese, but any one nationality is capped at 7% of those admitted. The large portion of Chinese (the full 7%) is noted as a national total, not a regional one. The Indian investor is the only mention of PR, the rest of the story does not focus on it.

PR has 6 EB-5 regional centers out of a national total of over 1300. EB-5 centers operate like thus. They are essentially a one stop shop for meeting the requirements of the EB-5 program. The money is given to the firm, and they invest it to make sure that the employment standards of EB-5 are met. They are not in any way associated with any foreign entity and do not look to be an effective way for China to implement belt and road. Of the six in PR, I could find only 3 with websites. The 6 centers in PR is not an outstanding number either, Nevada has 200,000 less people than PR but 8 centers instead of 6. Implementing any sort of concerted strategic buy up would be very difficult with this method. EB-5 does not seem to be connected to any belt-and-road strategic developments and industries.

The San Juan mall does not have significant evidence of direct Chinese investment. The mall was developed by Taubman Centers, a US based mall developer. The company does have a presence in China as well, though the vast majority of the operations are in the US. They have 3 mall centers in China as well as 1 in South Korea. These are administered by a Hong Kong based branch- Taubman Asia. This is the only bonafide Chinese connection to the San Juan Mall.

The largest petrochemical company in the world, Sinopec, has a presence on Puerto Rico. It is a State Subsidized Chinese company. It owns a US subsidiary called Puracap Caribe which operates in Puerto Rico. They have invested more than $50 Million since 2016, doubling employment and revving manufacturing by 600%

For: Alex Odishelidze
Prepared by: Alex Freeman
1/7/13

Jones Act Congressional Record Notes

I.   Congressional Record from January 30, 1917 - (CR 1.30.1917)

Pg. 2248 of Congressional Record (32 of PDF) - Discussion of "Government of Porto Rico" begins:

- Agreements on changing the wording of some amendments
    - o   Dealing with taxation, finances, separation of church and state, language, grammar

Pg. 2250 (34)

Mr. HARDING: I wish to ask the Senator from Colorado a question in relation to this section. Is it the intention of the sponsors of the bill to exempt all the subdivision and municipal bonds from Federal and State taxation?

Mr. SHAFROTH: I think that is the provision of the law.

Mr. HARDING: That is a provision that is not granted to any State in the Union.

Mr. SHAFROTH: It may be, but it is the same provision that we have extended to the Philippine Islands

[…]

Mr. SMOOT: I should like to ask the Senator if it would not be very much better to have the native of Porto Rico make a declaration that he desires to become a citizen of the United States; that is, to provide just the reverse of the proposition in the bill? Then a person who had not sufficient interest to become a citizen, or who is indifferent as to whether or not he is a citizen will not be covered into citizenship, unless he at least shows enough interest to make an application for citizenship.

Mr. SHAFROTH: I will state to the Senator from Utah that that matter has been the subject of a good deal of controversy in Porto Rico. When the island came into the possession of the United States the Porto Ricans all wanted to become citizens, and there was no protest. The Unionist Party, which is the strong party there, declared in favor of it. Afterwards, on account of certain differences, the Unionist Party declared for independence, and then they became violently opposed to coming into citizenship. Then there was a proposition which as presented here in Congress in favor of collective citizenship of the United States unless they file a declaration that they do not so desire.

[…]

Mr. SHAFROTH: Mr. President, I think the Senator from Utah will find that this provision is practically the provision which we have made in every similar instance. As I recollect, the only reason it was not done in the first instance was because of the fact that we had the Philippine proposition as the same time. They did not know exactly what they wanted to do.

Mr. SMOOT: I thought it very strange that we chould undertake to compel a person in Porto Rico, or in any territory over which we took control, to declare his intention not to become a citizen of the United States. I thought it would be very much better to have every one of them declare his intention to become a citizen of the United States. Then we should know that everyone who did so declare would at least have interest enough in the matter to become a citizen.

This conversation was the most pertinent I found in all 3 of the Debates in Congress. It continues as well for a few more paragraphs

Pg. 2251 (35)

- Debate whether majority of Porto Ricans desire independence or US citizenship.

Mr. VARDAMAN: If the question of independence were submitted to them, to choose between being a dependency of the United States or having their independence, I do not believe 1 per cent of them would vote to become part of the United States. If they should do otherwise they would prove themselves utterly unfit for citizenship in a free country, for a man who does not desire to be free and independent has not the elements of manhood in him essential to the making of a desirable citizen of this Republic.

Mr. GRONNA: That is exactly the way I understood the Senator from Mississippi. I was just going to say that it seems to me that it is not wise for us at this time to enact a law that will compel those people to become citizens of the United States, because that is not government by the consent of the governed.

- Debate continues whether Puerto Ricans desire to be Independent or part of the US, and their motivations for each side.

[…]

Mr. GRONNA: Mr. President, I have always believed that patriotism is what makes the citizen; that the mere fact of passing a bill or enacting a law does not make for good citizenship. Unless the people whom we make citizens desire to become a part of our great Government, unless patriotic motives move them to ask for this great privilege, I do not think that we are helping our Government by taking in a class of that kind.

- Debate to change length of time allowing Puerto Ricans to refuse citizenship to the US from 6 months to 1 year in order to allow all on the island fair chance to decide. Change upheld.

Pg 2252 (36)

- Discussion on military assets on the island to ensure strategic advantage of the Caribbean.
- Debate on language of lines of the bill.

Pg 2253-2265 (37-49)

- Debate on various amendments not relating to citizenship.

II.   Congressional Record from February 10, 1917 – (CR 2.10.1917)

Pg. 3005-3008 (31-34) – Discussion on "Government of Porto Rico" begins

- Debate on amendments that were not fully agreed upon from Jan. 30 debates.
- Debate on requirements to vote.

Pg. 3009 (35)

Mr. FALL: Mr. President, the trouble with this great United States to-day is the fact that we have among our numbers alien citizenship, not true American citizens. You say we are a melting pot for all nations of the earth. Yes, sir; and we have had an overdose of it. We have not been able to digest it.

Mr. MARTINE of New Jersey: Well, I have not seen any evidences of the evil of the melting pot. God knows, when I look out in New Mexico and over the arid plains of the West I think if a little of the dripping could have spread its way over there it would have been a blessing for every mortal within the borders of those States.

Pg. 3010-3011 (36-37)

- Debate on voting qualifications, taxes and the Governor's salary.

III.   Congressional Record from February 17, 1917 - (CR 2.17.1917)

Pg. 3467-3470 (1-4) – Discussion of "Government of Porto Rico" begins

- Discussion on voting requirements for Puerto Ricans

Pg 3470 (4)

[…]

Mr. FALL: Mr. President, we might just as well, it seems to me, understand that we are dealing with a condition which very few of us understand. We are providing here the utmost measure of self-government for the people of Porto Rico. In the very first place, those people have two aspirations. Divided very largely in two parties, they have had practical assurance from leaders of sentiment in the United States that they would never achieve either of their aspirations – one that it should become an independent republic and the other that it should get statehood. They have been told by leaders of both parties, by the leaders of sentiment as it is reported here in the United States, that they would neither become independent on the one hand, nor be allowed to enter the system of statehood upon the other.

Necessarily they differ when they come before a committee. They do not know what qualifications for voters they want, possibly, because it is possible the Republican Party, upon the one hand, has one ultimate object in view; the Union Party, upon the other, has confessedly another object in view; and the two attempting to achieve different ends have different ideas as to what should be embodied in a bill vesting in Porto Rico the right to self-government. I am frank to say that I think very few Members of the Senate understand what they are attempting to legislate about at all.

Pg 3471 (5)

- Continued discussion on qualifications to vote.

TESTIMONY OF ALEXANDER ODISHELIDZE

PLEBISCITE HEARINGS IN THE PUERTO RICO HOUSE OF REPRESENTATIVES

RELATING TO THE POLITICAL STATUS OF PUERTO RICO

I APPRECIATE THE OPPORTUNITY TO APPEAR IN FRONT OF THIS COMMITTEE TO EXPRESS MY PERSONAL OPINION RELATING TO THE ISSUE AS A LOCAL BUSINESSMAN OF 28 YEARS AND AUTHOR OF THE BOOKLET "PUERTO RICO AT THE CROSSROADS" (WHICH I AM OFFERING HERE AS PART OF THE RECORD ALONG WITH THE HEX REPORT).

THE TITLE OF MY BOOKLET, I FEEL, APPROPRIATELY EXPRESSES MY CONCERN OF THIS U.S. COLONY'S ECONOMIC FUTURE.

WE ARE INDEED AT A CROSSROADS, AND UNLESS WE RECOGNIZE THIS FINE POINT RIGHT NOW, WE MIGHT SLIP BACK INTO THE ECONOMIC STATUS OF BEING THE "POORHOUSE OF THE CARIBBEAN" AS WE WERE ONCE PRIOR TO 1950, REGARDLESS OF WHAT OUR OFFICIAL LABEL FOR OUR POLITICAL STATUS HAPPENS TO BE. "COMMONWEALTH" OR OTHERWISE.

AS I LOOK AROUND AND LISTEN TO THE DEBATE ABOUT THIS STATUS ISSUE, WHAT I HEAR MOSTLY IS CONFUSION ABOUT WHAT WE ARE AND WHO WE ARE.

THE U.S. HOUSE OF REPRESENTATIVES HAS CLEARLY STATED ON MARCH 4TH. 1998 THAT PUERTO RICO IS A TERRITORY OF THE U.S., THAT U.S. CONGRESS HAS THE ULTIMATE JURISDICTION OVER OUR FUTURE, AND THAT THIS CURRENT STATUS IS A TEMPORARY STATUS THAT CAN BE CHANGED BY CONGRESS AT ANY TIME AND PROBABLY WILL BE IN THE NOT TOO DISTANT FUTURE.

AND THE LOCAL ECONOMIC REALITIES ARE THAT OUR PER CAPITA INCOME IS 40% OF THE POOREST STATE OF THE U.S. AND THAT OUR UNEMPLOYMENT RATE RANGES BETWEEN 9% AND 24%. DOUBLE THAT OF THE MAINLAND U.S. I, AS A BUSINESSMAN, IF GIVEN THE OPPORTUNITY TO INVEST IN THIS TEMPORARY, UNCERTAIN SITUATION WOULD HESITATE TO DO SO UNLESS I HAD SOME SPECIAL CONCESSIONS. OR I HAD INSURANCE THAT WOULD TAKE CARE OF MY DOWNSIDE POLITICAL RISK, SUCH AS OPIC INSURANCE. BUT SINCE PUERTO RICO IS A U.S. TERRITORY, NO SUCH INSURANCE IS AVAILABLE FROM THE FEDERAL GOVERNMENT AS IT MIGHT BE FOR AN INVESTMENT IN GUATEMALA. THEREFORE, IT IS LESS RISKY TO INVEST IN GUATEMALA THAN

TO INVEST IN PUERTO RICO.

AS A RESULT, MOST OF THE INVESTMENT THAT PUERTO RICO HAS ENJOYED HAS BEEN ORIENTED AROUND A TAX GIMMICK.

AND OVER THE LAST FIFTEEN YEARS, BECAUSE THE ORIGINAL INVESTMENT WAS BASED ON THAT TAX GIMMICK, MORE CAPITAL FLOWED OUT OF PUERTO RICO THAN FLOWED IN (SEE P.R. AT THE CROSSROADS AND THE HEX REPORT).

THE OTHER LEG OF OUR ECONOMIC DEVELOPMENT HAS BEEN FEDERAL SOCIAL BENEFITS.

I HAVE SEEN STUDIES THAT SHOWED THAT EACH BILLION DOLLARS OF FEDERAL BENEFITS REPRESENTED APPROX. 50,000 JOBS. WE GET OVER $9 BILLION OF THOSE BENEFITS.

IF WE COMPARE THE JOB VALUE OF TAX GIMMICKS TO THE JOB VALUE OF WELFARE BENEFITS, IT IS EASY TO SEE WHICH SIDE OUR BREAD IS BUTTERED ON.

AND THAT IS OUR PROBLEM.

STAR IN THE CARIBBEAN"; PUERTO RICO.

AS A COLONY, WE CAN'T DEVELOP OUR OWN ECONOMIC DRIVERS. WE CAN'T DECIDE WHAT MINIMUM WAGES WILL APPLY WITHIN OUR OWN BORDERS. WE DON'T HAVE THE RIGHT TO USE OUR SHIPPING OF CHOICE. WE CAN'T ENTER INTO OUR OWN TAX TREATIES WITH OTHER COUNTRIES. OUR HANDS ARE TIED.

YET, AS A COLONY WE CANNOT ATTRACT THE KIND OF INVESTMENT THAT NORMALLY COMES TO STABLE POLITICAL JURISDICTIONS, ESPECIALLY STATES OF THE U.S.

TEMPORARY STATUS ONLY ATTRACTS TEMPORARY INVESTMENT. A PERMANENT STATUS, WITH SOVEREIGNTY, WILL CREATE SOLID ECONOMIC GROWTH BECAUSE IT WILL ATTRACT PERMANENT INVESTMENT.

WE CAN ACHIEVE SOVEREIGNTY THROUGH FREE ASSOCIATION WITH THE U.S. OR THROUGH ABSOLUTE INDEPENDENCE.

AND PERHAPS BECOME ANOTHER SINGAPORE WITH A PER CAPITA INCOME HIGHER THAN THE U.S.

OR WE CAN ACHIEVE THIS SOVEREIGNTY BY BECOMING A STATE OF THE U.S. AND HAVING A VOICE IN U.S. CONGRESS. STATISTICALLY, TERRITORIES THAT HAVE BECOME STATES HAVE ADDED OVER 3% TO THEIR GDP GROWTH. JUST LOOK AT ALASKA AND HAWAII.

EITHER WAY, WE WILL HAVE ACHIEVED PERMANENT STATUS WHICH WILL POSITION US TO ATTRACT INVESTMENT AND BUILD THAT SOLID ECONOMIC BASE.

THE TIME HAS COME TO STOP THINKING BLUE OR RED OR GREEN AND DEBATING WHETHER THERE IS OR ISN'T A BILATERAL PACT.

THE TIME HAS COME TO MAKE A CHOICE. BECAUSE IF WE HERE IN PUERTO RICO DON'T MAKE THIS CHOICE NOW, THE U.S. CONGRESS WILL MAKE THIS CHOICE FOR US LATER. AND I AM NOT SO SURE THEY WILL HAVE OUR BEST INTEREST IN MIND.

Chinese Investment in Puerto Rico

Title: Puerto Rico: The Land of Promise for Foreign Investors
Publisher: Telesur
https://www.telesurtv.net/english/news/Puerto-Rico-The-Land-of-Promise-for-Foreign-Investors-20180213-0030.html
Date: February 13, 2018

- The Yingke Caribbean China Center is looking to further invest in the construction of a massive cultural park, real estate management and medium cost housing development as well as numerous other endeavors in both the academic and scientific departments.
- Despite the fact that the island is still recovering from a devastating hurricane season, the CEO of Yingke Caribbean China Center, Jeff Carmichael, states, "there is no better time to be in Puerto Rico. It is not only because of the tax incentives but because of the beauty of the country, its people, the tremendous business opportunities."

Title: Yingke Caribbean China Center Opens in Puerto Rico
Publisher: Caribbean Business
http://caribbeanbusiness.com/yingke-caribbean-china-center-opens-in-puerto-rico%E2%80%A8%E2%80%A8/
Date: November 19, 2017

- Yingke Law Firm, China's largest law firm, has opened an office (the Yingke Caribbean China Center) in Puerto Rico to promote business and investment opportunities between China and Puerto Rico.

      ** Jeff Carmichael, the CEO of the Yingke Caribbean China Center, will be a guest speaker at the upcoming Puerto Rico Investment Summit in 2019

- According to the centers managing partner, the Yingke Caribbean China Center seeks to focus its economic resources and intellectual property in facilitating and coordinating external investments into Puerto.

    o They are particularly interested in infrastructure, clean renewable energy, healthcare, tourism and education, as well as direct investments in Puerto Rican companies focused on economic development in construction, manufacturing, senior housing, agriculture, export of products and services, and real estate.

- Yingke has already signed three memorandums of mutual understanding with Ciro Energy Group, Benítez Aviation and with Asia American Investments, Ltd.
    o Circo Energy Group: will promote a joint venture between the firm and Rosendin Electric, a large solar-power company, to facilitate renewable energy projects that are in the works and need capital.
    o Benítez Aviation: is aimed at broadening aviation services through the Caribbean.
    o Asia American Investments: seeks to identify the best local products for Chinese markets.

**Hurricane Maria makes landfall in Puerto Rico on September 20th 2017

Title: Bankrupt Caribbean Paradise Woos Chinese Tourists- and their Cash
Publisher: Bloomberg
https://www.bloomberg.com/news/articles/2017-08-30/chinese-tourists-and-cash-wooed-by-bankrupt-caribbean-paradise
Date: August 30, 2017

- Puerto Rico hopes to capitalize on China's new 'One Belt, One Road' infrastructure initiative that has already seen massive investments made in nearby Cuba and the Bahamas.
- An official delegation from Puerto Rico plans to visit China in late September following the first ever China-Puerto Rico Investment Forum which took place in early march.

  ** This visit never seems to have taken place, likely due to the anticipation/aftermath of Hurricane Maria

- Chinese investors have expressed interest in pharmaceuticals, tourism, manufacturing, power plants, road and bridge construction and recycling plants according to Puerto Rico's Economic Development Secretary Manuel Laboy-Rivera.
- PuraCap Caribe, a Chinese pharmaceutical company located in Puerto Rico, has invested more than $50 million since March 2016, doubling employment and increasing manufacturing more than 600 percent.
- Linda Yang, executive chairman of Yingke Global Holdings and a global partner in the associated Yingke Law Firm stated that "I really thought this could be a good place for Chinese investors." She also noted that "On the one hand, the bankruptcy gives some signals that there is some risk for this region. On the other hand, after the bankruptcy, it could be like a new start, a new start with many new opportunities."

Title: Manafort Still Doing International Work
Publisher: Politico
https://www.politico.com/story/2017/06/15/paul-manafort-fbi-trump-239573
Date: June 15, 2017

- The Chinese Development Fund, a subsidiary of the state-owned China Development Bank, consulted Manafort on a proposal to invest between $30-45 billion in the Puerto Rican government's bond debt and possibly the islands infrastructure. Manafort indicated that if the deal was made he could convince President Trump to sign on.
- Since May the deal seems to have died amidst concern on both sides.

Title: Chinese Culture Park to be Built
Publisher: El Nuevo Dia
https://www.elnuevodia.com/english/english/nota/chineseculturalparktobebuilt-2297486/
Date: March 4, 2017

- Yingke Global Holdings, a subsidiary of Yingke Law Firm, has signed an agreement with The Puerto Rican Government to invest $200 million dollars into a cultural and touristic center outside of San Juan.

- The center will span 200 acres and host a hotel, museums, restaurants, and workshops. At this time they believe the complex will be up and running by 2018/19.
- Congruent to this are plans to establish new Asian airline routs to Puerto Rico by 2020/21 with airlines such as Cathay Pacific, China Air, and Korean Air.
- The projections in the agreement state that, once the three phases are completed, the complex would receive 500,000 visitors per year, including 100,000 Chinese tourists through Yingke Tours, and it would have an annual economic impact of $1 billion.

**While I could not find anything to confirm this, it does seem as if plans to build the park were still in motion as of February 13, 2018 as per the telesur article.

Title: First China-Puerto Rico Forum Kicks Off
Publisher: Caribbean Business
http://caribbeanbusiness.com/first-china-puerto-rico-forum-kicks-off/
Date: March 1, 2017

- Puerto Rico is hosting the first China-Puerto Rico Investment Forum in March. The goal of the forum, which was organized by Yingke Law Firm, is to bring Chinese investments to Puerto Rico and the Caribbean.
- During the event, Gov. Ricardo Rosselló received the Distinguished Contribution Award between the United States and China, presented by the China U.S. Business Association. The award is given to an individual who "has had great achievements in their respective professional fields and has shown an unparalleled commitment and dedication to the ties and friendship between China and the United States." Former recipients include President George H.W Bush.
- Lavoy-Riviera, Secretary of the Economic Development and Commerce Department of Puerto Rico noted "Some 140 million Chinese visited the United States and, in 2017, that number will go up. We want to grab a market share of those millions that will be investing in and visiting the United States," Laboy Rivera said. "We want to capture that participation."
- Laboy said that the DDEC does not have numbers about how much Chinese investors have invested in Puerto Rico already.
- Laboy noted that "We do have some Chinese investment. There is a tire factory owned by a Chinese national in San Lorenzo. They do have a business presence. But now we want to do investments in a systematic way."
- The forum was attended by more than 150 Chinese investors and entrepreneurs.

Title: P.R to host 1st China Investment Forum Mar. 1-3
Publisher: News is my Business
Date: February 8, 2017

- Gov. Ricardo Rosselló wants to position Puerto Rico as an ideal investment destination for China. To that end, the governor has announced the first ever China-P.R investment forum from March 1-3.
- When announcing the forum the governor remarked "Puerto Rico is the ideal place for connecting China with the U.S. and Latin America. The dominance of Spanish and English

of Puerto Rican professionals is one crucial aspect to ensure the success of business between the two countries. Puerto Rico is open for business."

- "We must always aspire to be the gateway for Europe and Asia to Latin America," said Puerto Rico's Economic Development Secretary Manuel Laboy-Rivera.

Title: China Business Network Successfully Organized a Fam Trip to Puerto Rico
Publisher: China Invests
http://www.china-invests.net/20150518/36800.aspx
Date: May 18, 2015

- The Puerto Rico Tourism Company, Department of Economic Development and Commerce of Puerto Rico, and the China Business Network collaborated to bring a delegation of Chinese investors, tour operators, as well as a representative from China Central Television to Puerto Rico.
- The aim of the trip was to enhance the business and investment exchange between China and Puerto Rico.

Title: Puerto Rico Picks Bidders for Ailing Power Authority

Publisher: Wall Street Journal

https://www.wsj.com/articles/puerto-rico-picks-bidders-for-ailing-power-utility-11548000001

Date: January 20th, 2019

Puerto Rico Electric Power Authority has moved to privatize the island's power after the organization has fallen into debt, raised prices for consumers and been mismanaged. They took bidders. The four were : Duke Energy Corp. , ExelonCorp. , PSEG Services Corp. and a consortium of ATCO(Canadian) Ltd. , IEM Inc. and Quanta Services Inc. If a Chinese company buys the power distribution network on the island in the privatization, that could be a strong case for Chinese ambition in PR.

"FROM SKI TIPS TO STOCK TIPS"

a special program
sponsored by the Vail/Beaver Creek Ski School
A DAY ON THE SLOPES IMPROVING
YOUR SKIING AND SHARPENING
YOUR INVESTMENT ACUMEN

Join Alexander Odishelidze, certified ski instructor and nationally syndicated personal finance columnist and author, for an informal day of skiing and discussion. World economic and investment trends will be interspersed with ski tips. This leisurely day will include a gourmet lunch in one of Vail's finest restaurants.

PROGRAM INCLUDES:

- Day of ski instruction (terrain will include mostly groomed blue and green slopes)
- Gourmet Lunch (does not include alcoholic drinks)
- Discussion of personal finance issues and questions
- Copy of Mr. Odishelidze's book and audio tape, *"$... Making it and keeping it"*
- Six months subscription to Mr. Odishelidze's newsletter, *"Money Mastery"*

COST:

Private Seminars

$675 / one to three persons plus $125 for each additional person up to seven maximum. Available any time during Ski Season. Must be reserved and prepaid (Visa/MC) at least 24 hours in advance and is based on availability. Private session participants can meet either in front of Vail Village or Beaver Creek Ski School at 9:45 a.m. based on preference.

Beginning on Thursday, February 17 and every Thursday thereafter through February and March, this will be a regularly scheduled group seminar by the Vail/Beaver Creek Ski School.

Regularly Scheduled Group Seminars

$190 per person (maximum seven, minimum two)
You must be at least a level #5 skier. Participants can reserve ahead of time or depending on availability, just meet in front of Vail Village Ski School at 9:45 a.m. However, advance reservations are strongly recommended to assure your participation.

Comparable Value (if all the elements of the program were purchased separately) would exceed $350 per person based on seven participants. Cost of seminar may be tax deductible against investment income. Consult with your tax advisor regarding deductibility specifics.

Reserve your participation by calling Vail / Beaver Creek Ski School at 479-4330 or 1-800-237-8400 ext. 33 (24 hours per day, 7 days per week).

Para grupos privados este programa
se puede hacer en Español.

The Washington Post

Opinions

University rejects Chinese Communist Party-linked influence efforts on campus

By Josh Rogin Global Opinions January 14

As part of a broad effort to interfere in U.S. institutions, China tries to shape the discussion at American universities, stifle criticism and influence academic activity by offering funding, often through front organizations closely linked to Beijing.

Now that aspect of Beijing's foreign influence campaign is beginning to face resistance from academics and lawmakers. A major battle in this nascent campus war played out over the past six months at the University of Texas in Austin.

After a long internal dispute, a high-level investigation and an intervention by Sen. Ted Cruz (R-Tex.), the university last week rejected a proposal by the leader of its new China center to accept money from the China United States Exchange Foundation (CUSEF). The Hong Kong-based foundation and its leader, Tung Chee-hwa, are closely linked to the branch of the Chinese Communist Party that manages influence operations abroad.

The University of Texas debate erupted after the China Public Policy Center at the university's LBJ School of Public Affairs opened in August. Executive Director David Firestein proposed making CUSEF a principal funder of the initiative. Firestein, a former Foreign Service officer, had worked with the foundation before.

After several professors and university officials raised concerns about ties among CUSEF, Tung and the Communist Party, university President Gregory Fenves launched an investigation. Over several weeks, Fenves met with intelligence officials and experts to gauge the risk that accepting CUSEF money could compromise the university's academic integrity or give China undue access to and influence over academic products.

While the investigation was ongoing, Firestein held an event in November that was hosted by CUSEF and featured a former Chinese vice foreign minister. Shortly afterward, multiple reports highlighted that Tung is vice chairman of the Chinese People's Political Consultative Conference, a party organ that self-identifies as "a united front organization." The CPPCC and the Communist Party's United Front Work Department collaborate on China's influence operations abroad.

215

"The party's united front activities are intended — still described in Maoist terms — to mobilize the party's friends to strike at the party's enemies," said Peter Mattis, a China fellow at the Jamestown Foundation and former U.S. intelligence analyst. "That has no place on a university campus in America."

Tung was also the first chief executive of Hong Kong after the territory returned to Beijing's control. His foundation has funded research at many leading academic institutions and think tanks, including the Johns Hopkins University School of Advanced International Studies and the Brookings Institution. A CUSEF spokesman told me the foundation is not an agent of the Chinese government and is supported by private donors who believe a positive U.S.-China relationship "is essential for global well-being."

Before UT-Austin could become next on its list, Cruz weighed in. On Jan. 2, he warned Fenves in a letter that accepting CUSEF money could allow China to spread propaganda and compromise the university's credibility.

CUSEF and the United Front are the "external face" of the Communist Party's "internal authoritarianism," and giving them access to UT-Austin's education system could lead to "undue foreign influence and exploitation," Cruz wrote.

On Friday, Fenves told Cruz in a response that UT-Austin will not accept any funding from CUSEF for its China center. Before the senator's warning, the university had decided to reject "programmatic funding," Fenves wrote. After receiving the letter and inquiries from The Post, the university decided to ban all CUSEF funding.

Fenves shares Cruz's concerns that accepting CUSEF money "could create potential conflicts of interest or place limits on academic freedom and the robust exchange of ideas," he wrote. A Cruz aide said Fenves had preserved the integrity of the institution through his decision.

UT-Austin's decision has implications not only for the future of Chinese money in higher education but also for the greater effort to counter Chinese interference in free societies, known as "sharp power."

"This is one of the first examples of a university turning down money because it is tied to the Chinese Communist Party's united front activities," said Mattis, adding that the university's deliberative and informed process should be a model for other institutions.

Universities still face broader challenges in dealing with China. The Chinese government has sponsored hundreds of Confucius Institutes on college campuses that operate under opaque contracts and often stand accused of interfering in China-related education activities. Increasing numbers of Chinese students in the United States have come under pressure from their government when they have spoken against the party's narrative. Some have begun challenging professors who speak critically about Beijing's policies.

Due to the growing efforts of academics, government officials, lawmakers and journalists, the thin veil protecting organizations that do the Chinese Communist Party's bidding abroad is being peeled back. But the greater struggle to expose and then counter Chinese foreign interference in free societies is just beginning.

Mr. SMOOT. Mr. President, did the testimony before the committee show such a condition existing as that just pictured by the Senator from Mississippi, that not 1 per cent of the Porto Rican people would vote in favor of becoming citizens of the United States?

Mr. VARDAMAN. That was not stated in the testimony. There were some eloquent statements made before the committee. One young man appeared before the committee, with whom I was greatly impressed, who pleaded for the independence of Porto Rico, for the right to govern their own country, for the sanctity of their home that had been invaded and the sovereignty over which had been taken from them; but recognizing the fact, which any well-informed man who understands the Anglo-Saxon disposition in dealing with subject provinces will recognize, that independence is impossible, and since independence is not going to be given them, the majority of them expressed a desire to come in under the terms of this bill.

Mr. SMOOT. I asked the question of the Senator because I have received very many letters and petitions asking for the passage of legislation along this line, and also inclosing very many resolutions passed by organizations in Porto Rico—business organizations, religious organizations, and political organizations—and I thought from the correspondence that I have had and the information I have received that a great majority of the people of Porto Rico desired this legislation and preferred it even to independence.

Mr. VARDAMAN. Oh, I do not think that any of them do, but they realize that independence is impossible.

Mr. GRONNA. Mr. President, it is possible I may have misunderstood the statement of the distinguished Senator from Mississippi [Mr. VARDAMAN]; but if I interpret his statement correctly, it was to the effect that not to exceed 1 per cent of the Porto Ricans would vote to become citizens of the United States.

Mr. VARDAMAN. I stated that merely as my opinion. If the question of independence were submitted to them, to choose between being a dependency of the United States or having their independence, I do not believe 1 per cent of them would vote to become a part of the United States. If they should do otherwise they would prove themselves utterly unfit for citizenship in a free country, for a man who does not desire to be free and independent has not the elements of manhood in him essential to the making of a desirable citizen of this Republic.

Mr. GRONNA. That is exactly the way I understood the Senator from Mississippi. I was just going to say that it seems to me that it is not wise for us at this time to enact a law that will compel those people to become citizens of the United States, because that is not government by the consent of the governed.

Mr. SHAFROTH. Mr. President, if the Senator will allow me, I differ with the Senator from Mississippi with relation to that matter. There was a time when the parties to which I have referred insisted upon the right of independence, but since the European war broke out, and they see how helpless small nationalities are, they have ceased any agitation against this provision of the bill, and we have now in Washington representatives of the Unionist party and representatives of the Republican Party, both satisfied with this very provision of the bill. For that reason, I believe that the great mass of the people down there are in favor of this provision.

Mr. GRONNA. Well, Mr. President, that statement does not help the situation at all. That would be a matter of fear, and not a question of patriotism.

Mr. VARDAMAN. Mr. President, I will state, if the Senator will permit me, that, in my judgment, the conclusion reached by those people was brought about by our failure to give the Filipinos their independence. Those who have any intelligence realize that they are not going to be given their independence, and, since that is not going to be done, they prefer to have this bill. The Senator from Colorado is correct when he says that they would rather have this bill passed as it is than to live as they are living to-day. If, however, you will give them the slightest excuse for hope for independence, I repeat what I said, that I do not believe 1 per cent of them would prefer being a part, a subject province, of the United States to being independent; and it is perfectly natural that they should so feel; but if we do not enact this legislation now, our failure to do so will, I fear, serve to encourage those people to hope for the unattainable.

Mr. GRONNA. Or, in other words, we are simply giving them rights which they in fact will not exercise; we are giving them the same privileges that are given other citizens of the United States, privileges which, according to the statements of members of the committee, they never will accept or exercise.

Mr. SHAFROTH. I do not understand the Senator. I think, if voting is a test, that they will exercise the privileges accorded.

Over 250,000 vote there now. They have exercised the privileges accorded them and they want to retain the privileges which they have had all the time. So far as this provision is concerned, I am satisfied that they will not only consent to it, but that they will be glad to get it just as it has been written in the bill.

Mr. GRONNA. Well, Mr. President, we have had before us a bill which seeks to prevent certain people from entering our borders. Of course, I admit we are not under obligations to them as we are under obligations to the Porto Ricans, but under the immigration bill which we have had before us we exclude people who do want to come to our shores and who are anxious to become citizens of the United States. On the other hand, we are trying to pass a bill here to-night compelling the people of Porto Rico, unwilling though they may be, to become citizens of the United States.

Mr. President, I have always believed that patriotism is what makes the citizen; that the mere fact of passing a bill or enacting a law does not make for good citizenship. Unless the people whom we make citizens desire to become a part of our great Government, unless patriotic motives move them to ask for this great privilege, I do not think we are helping our Government by taking in a class of that kind.

Mr. HARDING. Mr. President—

The PRESIDING OFFICER. Does the Senator from North Dakota yield to the Senator from Ohio?

Mr. GRONNA. Yes; I yield to the Senator.

Mr. HARDING. I desire to ask the Senator from North Dakota if section 5 does not make it possible for any resident of Porto Rico to refrain from becoming a citizen if he so desires?

Mr. GRONNA. Yes; I understand that. But that is an entirely different thing. There may be many Porto Ricans who will not know in six months that a law has been passed by the United States Congress making them citizens of the United States, whether they want to be citizens or not.

Mr. HARDING. If that be true, I do not think it will make very much difference to such a citizen to what Government he gives his allegiance.

Mr. GRONNA. Then, I want to ask the Senator is that the character of people that we want to have as citizens of the United States?

Mr. HARDING. Well, in the uplifting work in which this Government is engaging I think it is becoming for us to make worthy people of such as we can.

Mr. GRONNA. We have just been dealing with the aborigines of this country, the American Indians, and we are complaining because we have to provide appropriations of public funds to civilize them and to educate them. We have heard a great deal of complaint on that account on this floor within the last few days. Now, we are taking in all classes of people and providing that anyone who lives in this country and on this island, whether it is a Jap or whether it is an Asiatic belonging to any other country, shall be a citizen of the United States.

Mr. President, I shall not, of course, object—it would make very little difference whether I should object or not—but I want at least to give these people a year to think it over. Six months is not sufficient time; and I desire to ask the Senator from Colorado if he would object to striking out "six months" and providing that the time shall be 12 months?

Mr. SHAFROTH. I accept that amendment. It is perfectly satisfactory.

Mr. GRONNA. I make that suggestion.

The PRESIDING OFFICER. The amendment will be stated.

The SECRETARY. On page 7, line 13, it is proposed to strike out "six months" and insert "one year."

The amendment was agreed to.

Mr. SHAFROTH. Also in line 22 of the same page.

Mr. GRONNA. Yes; that is right.

The SECRETARY. It is also proposed, in line 22, to strike out "six months" and insert "one year."

The amendment was agreed to.

Mr. GRONNA. Also in line 24.

The SECRETARY. In line 24, page 7, the same amendment is proposed.

The amendment was agreed to.

Mr. SHAFROTH. Also in line 3 of page 8.

The SECRETARY. On page 8, line 3, it is proposed to strike out "six months" and insert "one year."

The amendment was agreed to.

The reading of the bill was resumed, and the Secretary read to the end of section 7, the last section read being as follows:

SEC. 7. That all property which may have been acquired in Porto Rico by the United States under the cession of Spain in the treaty of peace entered into on the 10th day of December, 1898, in any public bridges, road houses, water powers, highways, unnavigable streams and the beds thereof, subterranean waters, mines or minerals under the surface of

I think it might be clarified, and there is some little doubt about it. If we do not get through the bill to-night, there will be time to rectify it.

Mr. SHAFROTH. That will be satisfactory.

Mr. HARDING. I wish to ask the Senator from Colorado a question in relation to this section. Is it the intention of the sponsors of the bill to exempt all the subdivision and municipal bonds from Federal and State taxation?

Mr. SHAFROTH. I think that is the provision of the law.

Mr. HARDING. That is a provision that is not granted to any State in the Union.

Mr. SHAFROTH. It may be, but it is the same provision that we have extended to the Philippine Islands.

Mr. VARDAMAN. If the Senator from Ohio will yield to me for a moment, in the consideration of this bill it was thought that this special exemption should be given in order to make this security as attractive as possible. Those people there are undeveloped, and it is for the purpose of enabling them to develop their country to make the securities attractive by extending that exemption. It was thought by the committee that it would probably be better for those people.

Mr. HARDING. I have no insistent objection. I wondered if the reading of the section was clear; that is all.

The PRESIDING OFFICER. Without objection, the section will go over until to-morrow.

Mr. SMOOT. I should like to ask the Senator if it would not be very much better to have the native of Porto Rico make a declaration that he desires to become a citizen of the United States; that is, to provide just the reverse of the proposition in the bill? Then a person who had not sufficient interest to become a citizen, or who is indifferent as to whether or not he is a citizen, will not be covered into citizenship, unless he at least shows enough interest to make an application for citizenship.

Mr. SHAFROTH. I will state to the Senator from Utah that that matter has been the subject of a good deal of controversy in Porto Rico. When the island came into the possession of the United States the Porto Ricans all wanted to become citizens, and there was no protest. The Unionist Party, which is the strong party there, declared in favor of it. The Unionist Party declared for independence, and then they became violently opposed to coming into citizenship. Then there was a proposition which was presented here in Congress in favor of collective citizenship; that is, that all Porto Ricans should come into citizenship of the United States unless they file a declaration that they do not so desire.

Mr. FALL. Mr. President——

The PRESIDING OFFICER. Does the Senator from Colorado yield to the Senator from New Mexico?

Mr. SHAFROTH. I yield.

Mr. FALL. Has it not been the universal custom of the United States in the acquisition of any territory to embody exactly this provision in the treaty of acquisition? It was so in the case of Louisiana in 1803, of Florida in 1819, of New Mexico and California and Arizona and Texas in 1846. In the treaties and in the organic acts with reference to the acquisition of any of that territory there has been just this provision.

Mr. SHAFROTH. I think that is true.

Mr. FALL. All residents there were regarded as citizens of the United States, unless within a limited period of time they declared their intention to remain citizens of some other country.

Mr. SMOOT. There is, of course, this difference: In all the cases which the Senator from New Mexico has mentioned the territory was a part of this continent, adjoining the United States, and it became a part of the United States through purchase or otherwise. Does the Senator from New Mexico remember how it was as to any territory outside the continental limits of the United States?

Mr. FALL. There was the acquisition of Hawaii.

Mr. SMOOT. How was it as to Hawaii?

Mr. FALL. The residents of Hawaii all came in as citizens of the United States. Even the Japanese who were born in Hawaii are citizens of the United States. They are now increasing there much more rapidly than any other race we have there.

Mr. SMOOT. They constitute more than half of all the people of the island.

Mr. FALL. They will soon have control there. We shall soon have Japanese Delegates in the Congress of the United States.

Mr. SMOOT. I do not think there is any doubt about that.

Mr. SHAFROTH. Mr. President, I think the Senator from Utah will find that this provision is practically the provision which we have made in every similar instance. As I recollect,

the only reason it was not done in the first instance was because of the fact that we had the Philippine proposition at the same time. They did not once exactly what they wanted to do.

Mr. SMOOT. I thought it very strange that we should undertake to compel a person in Porto Rico, or in any territory over which we took control, to declare his intention not to become a citizen of the United States. I thought it would be very much better to have every one of them declare his intention to become a citizen of the United States. Then we should know that everyone who did so declare would at least have interest enough in the matter to become a citizen.

Mr. FALL. The theory upon which this Government has ever acquired any further territory has always been that it proposed to erect sovereign States of the Union in that territory as soon as they were fitted for statehood. That has been the universal custom from time immemorial until the acquisition of the Philippine Islands after the war with Spain. It has been the universal custom to incorporate all the inhabitants in the acquired territory immediately as citizens of the United States, except where by treaty provision the mother country ceding that country to the United States required us to allow its citizens the privilege of remaining citizens of the country from which the territory was acquired, in the event they so desired.

For that reason, as I say, in the treaty by which we acquired Louisiana in 1803, Florida in 1819, and the Mexican territory in 1846, the mother country in each instance agreed by treaty that those who did not desire to become citizens of the United States should have the privilege of remaining citizens of France or of Spain or of Mexico, as the case might be. Those who did not within one year—which has been the period heretofore limited—file a declaration of intention to remain citizens of the foreign country became incorporated immediately as citizens of the United States. Of course it was all upon the theory that eventually those Territories were to be erected into States.

Mr. VARDAMAN. Mr. President, in the hearings before the committee when it had under consideration this bill I was very much impressed by some of the Porto Ricans who came before the committee and gave testimony. I do not think there was one of them who did not deep down in his patriotic heart cherish the hope that some day his country might be an independent sovereign political entity; and down deep in my heart I sympathized with him. I do not think any man, however good he may be, is good enough to govern another man without that man's consent. I know the United States are not good enough to govern Porto Rico without Porto Rico's consent.

So far as I am personally concerned, I really think it is a misfortune for the United States to take that class of people into the body politic. They will never, no, not in a thousand years, understand the genius of our government or share our ideals of government; but the United States has taken this island; the investments that have been made there by American white men will induce the Government to continue to hold it; and if the island is going to become a part of this Republic, I do not see any other way to treat the inhabitants thereof. It is very much more convenient to do it in this way, by one drag-net act, than it would be to require them to come individually and to make their requests to be made a part of the Government or to be made citizens of the United States.

We considered that matter carefully, and while I have no desire in the world to coerce them, I really had rather they would not become citizens of the United States. I think we have enough of that element in the body politic already to menace the Nation with mongrelization; but if the Porto Ricans are going to be held against their will, as we are holding them now, then we ought to legislate for their interests. We should make the coercion as palatable as possible.

Mr. FALL. It is our duty to give them some citizenship, is it not?

Mr. VARDAMAN. I agree with the Senator that we ought to do that if we are going to hold them. We have taken them against their will; we are holding them now against their will. If it were submitted to a vote, there would not be 1 per cent who would vote in favor of becoming a part of these United States.

Mr. FALL. We have deprived them, however, of the protection of Spain. They can no longer appeal to their mother country as Spanish citizens; they can not appeal to the United States to-day as American citizens; they can not appeal, of course, to Porto Rico, because Porto Rico can not enforce their rights anywhere in the world they may go. We have placed these people in the most anomalous position that the people of almost any country were ever placed in; they are citizens of no country.

Mr. VARDAMAN. Absolutely; and I do not think that the natives there are getting what they are entitled to.

For: Alex Odishelidze
By: Alex Freeman
3/10/13

A Civil Government for Porto Rico Hearings Notes

First Session on HR 8501 – January 13 and 15, 1916

Speakers: Rep. William A. Jones, Virginia, Chairman; Arthur Yager, Governor of Porto Rico;
Rep. Luis Munoz Rivera, Porto Rico; Rep. Clarence R. Miller, Minnesota

Pg. 7 – Discussion on granting US citizenship to Puerto Ricans

Gov. YAGER: None at all; and there is no reason on earth why we should not make any people whom we have permanently attached to our country citizens. They owe allegiance and obey the laws and are open to all the pains and penalties imposed for their disobedience. Of course, this does not imply suffrage or statehood. It does not imply anything except just what it says.

The CHAIRMAN: Now, Governor, what is the sentiment of the Porto Rican people themselves in regard to this questions of citizenship? How do they feel about it: what do they want?

Gov. YAGER: I have no hesitation myself in saying that the great body of the Porto Rican people want citizenship in the United States. The question has had an unfortunate history, because of the delay in granting it. At the start everybody in Porto Rico though they were going to be made citizens, and as to that they were made citizens of Porto Rico –whatever that means- and that made them feel discouraged, and it suggested to them that if they are citizens of Porto Rico there ought to be an independent Porto Rico for them to be citizens of. And some of them began to dream then of independence and some took up the idea that citizenship would interfere with independence, and they did not want to be citizens of the United States, but wanted everything arranged looking toward independence. That has passed away. The feeling now is, with the masses of the Porto Rican people, that they would cheerfully accept citizenship with some increased participation in their own government there at home, which they, of course, think is impolite in the words "citizenship of the United States."

The CHAIRMAN: What action has been taken by the political parties in Porto Rico recently upon this subject?

Gov. YAGER: [...] As I understand it, that party used to be in favor of independence; that is, as an ultimate goal for Porto Rico, and they had that plank in their platform, and stood for independence as the ultimate destiny of the island. Recently that party has had a convention and changed its platform and put such limitations upon its leaders that those who were absolutely committed to independence and nothing else had to retire from positions of influence in the party and give it an entirely new propaganda- that is, for self-government; that is, for larger participation for Porto Ricans in their own government, but without any agitation against American control.

[...]

Pg. 9

Mr. MILLER: [...] I understand that formerly there was an agitation for citizenship, as you just stated.

Gov. YAGER: Yes, sir; early in the history of our connection with the island.

Mr. MILLER: When we had the bill up two years ago there was a hearing on the bill and they did not want citizenship, but independence. Was that change due to the change in the administration here? You will remember that the freedom of the Philippines was talked of and did they not think that it would be a good thing to have it passed all around?

Gov. YAGER: Possibly, but I really do not think so. I think that the independence movement in Porto Rico was built up upon the foundation of rather a sentimental attitude, caused by the denial of citizenship, and the cause of it was a political matter. The politicians took great interest in the appointment of a certain official there. That official was not appointed. An American was appointed instead, and that just furnished the match to the fuse. They are a very sentimental people. They can get up a very strong excitement in a few minutes about matters of really no great importance. That is the Latin-American temperament, and so they exploded and went off rapidly and committed themselves in general to a propaganda for independence; then, having gone off, it is not always easy to get back; but they have gotten back.

[...]

Mr. MUNOZ RIVERA: As regards to the question of citizenship, I wish to make my position as clear as possible. I am the only representative of Porto Rico in this Congress, and it is my duty to record here the various views of my countrymen on the subject. [...]

I can safely say that not a single Unionist entertains any feeling of hostility toward the United States; on the contrary, every one of them recognizes the fact that the people of Porto Rico owe a debt of profound gratitude to the United States for the progress made on the island under the American flag, and they hope that as the years go by this progress will increase.

Session on HR 8501 – February 5, 1916

Speakers: Mr. M. Rodriguez Serra, Civic Association of Porto Rico; Rep. William A. Jones, Virginia, Chairman; Rep. Harvey Helm, Kentucky; Mr. Cayetano Coll Cuchi, Representative from the Union Party in Puerto Rico;

Pg. 3

Excerpt from "Statement of Mr. M. Rodriguez Serra," a representative of the Civic Association of Porto Rico

Mr. SERRA: [...] The most important question for us is that of citizenship. We consider it a great honor to be citizens of the United States. We have no unfriendly feelings toward this great country. On the contrary, those among us who have had the fortune of acquiring some knowledge of your glorious history have felt and feel deep admiration and regard for the Nation which justly has deserved the title of champion of liberty and human rights.

But we want to preserve our present political status, or condition, which was created by Congress as provided for in section 7 of the organic law now in force. As we understand or interpret it, we are a body politic, known as the people of Porto Rico with certain governmental powers, very restricted, through with our own Porto Rican citizenship, and entitled to the protection of the United States. We are not incorporated into your Nation, we belong to no other nation, yet we are a body politic within your protection. Perhaps it might be correct to say that we are a protectorate of the United States.

We want to continue in that situation, because under it we may develop, we may obtain an enlargement of our government powers, until the ties binding us to your Nation, by your will, disappear, and we might become absolutely independent.

[...] (pg 4)

Not only do we desire, as a question of natural sentiment - and sentiment is the salt of the earth – to preserve our own collective personality – that is to say, our system of legislation, our culture, traditions, language, customs, good habits – which, as you know, make up the spiritual character of a nation; we are anxious besides to have the power, the political power, independent of any foreign sovereignty, to be able to meet and solve our economic situation, which to speak in all candor, has grown worse and worse since our island fell under the jurisdiction of the United States.

[...]

With the acquisition of Porto Rico by the United States we lost the fruits of our political efforts of several decades. A military government was first established, and then the present organic act was enacted, in 1900. No progressive reform was ever afterwards adopted by Congress. We continued unanimously clamoring for home rule. Our people began to be disappointed, and at the same time our thinking men endeavored to study the problem of our ultimate permanent destiny. We soon reached the conclusion that nobody from the outside could understand our problems like ourselves. ... No question, then, that under the law of God Porto Rico belongs to the Porto Ricans.

[...] (pg 6)

"We are developing a real deep intense nationalistic tendency, which is bound to grow and become stronger as the time passes. Nobody can say that such a feeling or tendency will be crushed by virtue of a law."

Pg. 12

Mr. AUSTIN: And they sent you before this committee to ask for an independent form of government?

Mr. SERRA: No, sir. As I explained in the beginning, I represent three associations –The Civic Association of Porto Rico, the Latin-American Association, the Antillian Union, and the Bar Association of Porto Rico. I represent three associations that ask for independence. The bar association asked me to come here to ask only for suppression or discontinuance of the United States District Court for Porto Rico.

Pg. 18

Mr. SERRA: We are developing a collective personality that should not be destroyed. The people of Porto Rico are asserting themselves more and more every day. We have our own culture, our own system of legislation, and our own customs. We are isolated, we are a nation of our own, and we do not want to be destroyed.

Mr. AUSTIN: Suppose we turn you loose and some other government wants you. How would you protect yourselves then?

Mr. SERRA: We will submit to fate.

Pg. 30

The CHAIRMAN: I want to understand your position. Is this your position: Until the United States declares definitely and positively what your future political status shall be you would rather that this bill should not say anything on the subject of citizenship? You would like to have that question left in abeyance until Congress has decided definitely and positively whether you are to remain as a Territorial possession or whether you are at some time in the future to become a State of the United States?

Mr. CUCHI: Exactly.

[...]

Pg. 31

Mr. CUCHI: I will give you my opinion, and that is that we are under the present Foraket Act citizens of the United States.

[...]

Pr. 32

Mr. HELM: You think your present status as citizens would justify or authorize the President of the United States to select consuls to these Central American Governments as accredited representatives of this Government to transact governmental business?

Mr. CUCHI: I think it would.

Mr. HELM: Is there any questions in your mind about it?

Mr. CUCHI: Not at all. As a legal proposition, the United States is the only power that would have control of the citizen. No nation could question the act of the United States. The mere fact of the appointment will carry with it the full weight and force of citizenship. Inasmuch as there is a law of Congress that says for international purposes Porto Ricans are considered citizens of the United States. If Porto Ricans were injured in Europe, I have no doubt that the United States would be back of them.

[...]

Mr. HELM: The purpose of my question is to bring out the actual status of citizenship.

Mr. CUCHI: It would be a very fine thing. Unquestionably, the Supreme Court would have to pass upon it.

Mr. HELM: Personally, I am very much interested in your particular proposition. I would like to see as many of the consuls and representatives of the United States selected from Porto Rico as possible, because I believe that is the most efficient way to transact our business in Central and Latin America.

Session on S. 1217 – March 22, 1916

Speakers: Sen. John F. Shafrtoth, Colorado, Chairman; Mr. Samuel Gompers, President of the American Federation of Labor

The whole hearing debates the rights of workers in Puerto Rico, detailing labor conditions, strikes and the local government's response.

Further Reading on Puerto Rico

Below is a list of recent articles written about Puerto Rico's status, economy, and geopolitical future. I hope you find them informative. While many of these articles are unbiased, you will find that some have been influenced by certain factions with specific agendas. With this in mind, I encourage you to read with a careful eye.

Cheatham, Amelia. "Puerto Rico: A US Territory in Crisis." *Council on Foreign Relations*, https://www.cfr.org/backgrounder/puerto-rico-us-territory-crisis.

"Statement by President Joseph R. Biden, Jr. on Puerto Rico." *The White House*, https://www.whitehouse.gov/briefing-room/statements-releases/2021/06/07/statement-by-president-joseph-r-biden-jr-on-puerto-rico/

Conde, Zayira Jordán. "Puerto Rico Statehood Will Help Protect Democracy in the Region." *Newsweek*, https://www.newsweek.com/puerto-rico-statehood-will-help-protect-democracy-region-opinion-1616595.

de Jesús, Federico and Laura Rodriguez. "An Urgent Rescue Plan for Puerto Rico." *The Center for American Progress*, https://www.americanprogress.org/article/urgent-rescue-plan-puerto-rico/.

Nwanevu, Osita. "The Vexing Question of Puerto Rican Statehood." *The New Republic*, https://newrepublic.com/article/162222/puerto-rico-statehood-velasquez-aoc.

Serrallés, Jorge Cruz. "What Does Puerto Rico Cost the US?" *Medium*, https://medium.com/@jorgecruzserralles/what-does-puerto-rico-cost-the-us-c179304bab93

Coto, Dánica."US Fights Ruling to Extend SSI Benefits to Puerto Rico." *U.S. News*, https://www.usnews.com/news/us/articles/2021-06-07/us-fights-ruling-to-extend-ssi-benefits-to-puerto-rico

"Puerto Rico - Economic Indicators." *Moody's Analytics*, https://www.economy.com/puerto-rico/indicators

Cabán, Pedro. "The End of the Commonwealth of Puerto Rico." *Dissent Magazine*, https://www.dissentmagazine.org/online_articles/the-end-of-the-commonwealth-of-puerto-rico

"The Biden-Harris Plan for Recovery, Renewal and Respect for Puerto Rico." *JoeBiden.com*, https://joebiden.com/the-biden-harris-plan-for-recovery-renewal-and-respect-for-puerto-rico/

Garrett, R. Sam. "Political Status of Puerto Rico: Brief Background and Recent Developments for Congress." *Congressional Research Service*, https://sgp.fas.org/crs/row/R44721.pdf.

Sutter, John D. and Sergio Hernandez. "'Exodus' from Puerto Rico: A visual guide." *CNN Investigates,* https://www.cnn.com/2018/02/21/us/puerto-rico-migration-data-invs/index.html.

Hackett, Ashley. "Young Puerto Ricans Are Leaving the Island to Escape the Territory's Debt." *Pacific Standard*, https://psmag.com/social-justice/young-puerto-ricans-are-leaving-the-island-to-escape-the-territorys-debt.

Newkirk II, Vann R. "Puerto Rico's Dire Health-Care Crisis." *The Atlantic*, https://www.theatlantic.com/politics/archive/2017/10/puerto-ricos-health-care-crisis-is-just-beginning/544210/.

Nelson, Eshe. "Puerto Rico's eye-popping economic situation, in charts." *Quartz*, https://qz.com/1091341/puerto-ricos-eye-popping-economic-situation-in-charts/.

Setser, Brad W. "What Exactly is in the New Agreement Between Puerto Rico's Board and its Creditors?" *Council on Foreign Relations*, https://www.cfr.org/blog/what-exactly-new-agreement-between-puerto-ricos-board-and-its-creditors.

Hillman, Jennifer and David Sacks. "China's Belt and Road: Implications for the United States." *Council on Foreign Relations*, https://www.cfr.org/report/chinas-belt-and-road-implications-for-the-united-states/.

"2017 Puerto Rican status referendum." *Wikipedia,* https://en.wikipedia.org/wiki/2017_Puerto_Rican_status_referendum#:~:text=A%20referendum%20on%20the%20political,overwhelmingly%20chose%20statehood%20by%2097%25.

"2020 Puerto Rican status referendum." *Wikipedia*, https://en.wikipedia.org/wiki/2020_Puerto_Rican_status_referendum.

About the Author

A Russian-Georgian born in Belgrade, Serbia, **Alexander Odishelidze** survived the Nazi occupation of Yugoslavia and the Holocaust. Despite losing his family and being shipped to refugee camps in Europe, Odishelidze grew into a strong, intelligent, and driven man. Immigrating to America with no grasp of the English language, no friends, and only twenty dollars in his pocket, he was drafted into the United States Army, where he trained in Alaska and became an expert skier. But his dreams and ambitions evolved.

Upon leaving the Army, Odishelidze began his career in financial services and became the youngest ever general manager of a prestigious MONY financial services operation in Manhattan, New York. In 1971, Odishelidze began insurance and securities operations in Puerto Rico, until Aetna bought them out in 1985. He formed Eba, Inc. in 1979, as a consulting subsidiary, which he continued in Puerto Rico, and formed his financial and political consulting firm, Omanagement, LLC, in 2008 for his U.S. mainland operations. He's a guru in his field, writing columns, newsletters, and books on finance. Odishelidze and his wife, Odette Bouret, spend their time between their homes in Florida, St. John, and Colorado.

Index

A

Acabá, Joseph Michael "Joe," 76
Anthony, Mark, 76
al-Assad, Bashar, 5
audits in Puerto Rico, 42–43

B

Belt and Road Initiative, 5–6,
    69, 71
Berríos, Rubén, 35
Biden, Joe, 12, 64
Boom and Bust in Puerto Rico
    (Maldonado), 55–56
Burton, Dan, 51–52
Bush, George W., 3

C

China
    Belt and Road Initiative, 5–6,
        69, 71
    foreign policy goals, 73
    Latin American invest-
        ments, 6–7
    Puerto Rico investments, 6–10
    Roosevelt Roads purchase ne-
        gotiations, 2–5

Churchill, Winston, 3
citizenship for Puerto Ricans,
    20–21, 72
Clinton, Bill, 51
Clinton, Hillary, 12
colonial status of Puerto Rico, 69
Columbus, Christopher, 19
"Confronting the China Challenge"
    (US Council on Foreign
    Relations Transition 2020
    Series), 73
Confucius, 31
Congressional lobbying efforts for
    Young Bill, 45–52
constitution (Puerto Rico), 24
controlled foreign corporations
    (CFCs), 36–38, 67–69
Council on Foreign Relations, 17
COVID-19 pandemic, 70
Craig, Larry, 51
Cuba
    Chinese investment in, 7
    purchase of, 19–20
Culebra, 4

CPSIA information can be obtained
at www.ICGtesting.com
Printed in the USA
LVHW042302060323
741047LV00001B/201